COMPULSIVE SPY

COMPULSIVE SPY

THE STRANGE CAREER OF E. HOWARD HUNT

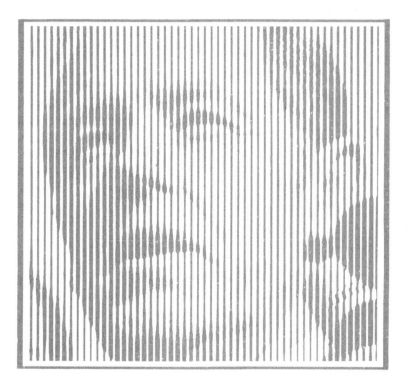

TAD SZULC

THE VIKING PRESS | NEW YORK

Photograph on title page by Wide World.

THIS BOOK IS FOR MATTHEW Q.

CONTENTS

AUTHOR'S NOTE

This is an incomplete story of a man whose life and ultimate fate remain unresolved. E. Howard Hunt, Jr., is part of the story of Watergate and the Nixon Presidency. As such, he is part of American history—still in the making. This sketch of Howard Hunt cannot even aspire to the category of a definitive biography —by nature and by dint of his professional life Hunt is elusive. I met him only once, during the preparations for the 1961 Bay of Pigs invasion, and even that encounter was brief and superficial. So this is a reconstruction, from a distance, about a man whom I find fascinating in the context of our time.

It is customary to acknowledge the assistance of those who made possible the writing of a book. I have received no official help—from the Central Intelligence Agency or the White House— nor did I expect it. The help I did receive came from past and present CIA and State Department officials and others. I am grateful for their time and their patience in aiding to guide me through that period of our history running from the late 1940s to date. They will recognize their own contributions to this book.

As for source material, I have drawn heavily on the published daily work of my professional colleagues in the craft of journalism—especially those on *The Washington Post* and *The New York Times*—as well as on transcripts of testimony and hearings before grand juries and Congressional panels.

Howard Hunt's own books were, of course, essential in attempting to understand him. I have read nine of his forty-five novels and his own account of the Bay of Pigs. To understand the psychological framework in which the CIA—and Howard Hunt— operated in the 1950s and the early 1960s, I found *The Craft of Intelligence* by the late Allen W. Dulles to be invaluable. For understanding the contemporary Washington context, even before Watergate, *The Politics of Lying* by David Wise is an important book.

Finally, I am indebted to my publisher, Thomas Guinzburg, and my editor at The Viking Press, Elisabeth Sifton, for their judgment that this book should be written at this time. This judgment was shared by my literary agent and friend, Carl D. Brandt. And I must record the fact that the actual production of the manuscript was immensely helped by my daughter, Nicole, who coordinated all the research material, carried out several key interviews for me, and transcribed innumerable tapes during a frantic stretch of sleepless nights. My wife assured us of the peace and quiet in which the work could be done.

Washington, D. C.
October 10, 1973

THE BACKDROP

1

Watergate—the symbolic shorthand word we use to describe the great political scandals of the early 1970s—was not born in a vacuum. The men who planned, ordered, and executed the Watergate crimes were neither the product of nor a sudden aberration in American history. Both Watergate and those associated with it were, instead, the result of a strange American historical process with roots in the early years of the Cold War.

This process culminated in a plan, first conceived in Richard M. Nixon's White House in 1970, to apply Cold War techniques of foreign intelligence operations to political surveillance, espionage, and sabotage against Americans at home. Watergate, therefore, was actually launched in July 1970, when President Nixon approved a top-secret plan for domestic intelligence operations, although the psychological climate for it had existed for a long time among the men who thought it up.

Watergate foundered on June 17, 1972, almost two years later, when, through a sheer accident of carelessness on the part of the chief "dirty tricks" operator, the five men arrested after breaking into the Washington headquarters of the Democratic National Committee could be linked with the White House.

Nations are often saved or disgraced by seemingly unimportant events, barely understood at the time of their occurrence. This was the case with the 1972 Watergate raid. Looking back, we may be thankful that what the White House at first contemptuously called a "third-rate burglary" *did* happen on that June night, and that the raiders were caught red-handed—because it exposed and, I hope, killed the great conspiracy of domestic intelligence and other secret and sinister enterprises that otherwise might have veered the United States in the direction of becoming a corrupt police state.

This is not a history of Watergate and/or of its ramifications. The full story of Watergate has not yet run its course. Its extraordinary political consequences are certain to be felt for years to come. My overriding interests in this account are the conditions and the circumstances which over long years produced the men—and the state of mind—that could embark with such frightening enthusiasm upon the Watergate adventures. The philosophy and the personality of President Nixon are not the subject of this inquiry, nor is the outlook of high officials in his administration who, with or without his total knowledge of all the operational details, joined in the conspiracy of the 1970s. Such an analysis must be left to future historians. I do believe, however, that the spirit of Watergate can be perceived and captured through the life and the times of one single man—most of whose life was spent enveloped in the anonymity of undercover intelligence work, but who suddenly burst upon the national scene as the personification of all the painful things symbolized by Watergate.

He is E. Howard Hunt, Jr., sentenced to a provisional 35-year prison term, whose careless slip on June 17, 1972, led to the ultimate exposure of most of the Watergate scandals. He had been the chosen, or perhaps one should say the ill-chosen, instrumentality of this conspiracy. What Hunt, a retired Central Intelligence Agency clandestine operative, did before, during, and after the Watergate affair tells us a great deal about the very special Cold War environment from which he came. It explains to an important extent his actions in the context of Watergate, and, I think, it provides considerable insight into the atmosphere that pervaded Washington after President Nixon took office in 1969 and set in motion the forces that blossomed darkly in Watergate. Without the Howard Hunts of this world the operations visualized by the White House and the Committee for the Re-Election of the President in 1971 and 1972 could not have happened.

But was Hunt typical? Was he a unique personality? In the judgment of his peers and superiors in the CIA, which he faithfully but often erratically served for twenty-two of his fifty-three years, his age at the time of the Watergate break-in, Hunt was far from being the only one of his breed. There are other Hunts in the CIA, still on active service or in retirement, as there are other Hunts in other segments of American life. G. Gordon Liddy, an ex-agent of the Federal Bureau of Investigation and Hunt's partner in the White House's secret Special Investigative Unit, seems to have had the same mentality, the same viewpoint, and the same peculiar philosophy as Howard Hunt. So did Tom Charles Huston, Nixon's youthful aide, who drafted the "For Eyes Only" plans for "expanded" domestic intelligence operations after meeting with the President, his top advisers, and heads of all the intelligence agencies. The cast of mind represented by Huston is best illustrated in passages from his top-secret recommendations to the President.

Huston's notion, evidently encouraged by Nixon, was that existing constitutional and legal restraints on domestic intelligence operations—the restraints designed to protect the rights of Americans—could and should be removed in the interest of what the White House perceived to be "national security." I think it is useful to quote from Huston's memorandum to the President to get the flavor of what was being proposed:

Present procedures should be changed to permit intensification of coverage of individuals and groups in the United States who posed a major threat to the internal security. . . . The restrictions on legal coverage [Huston was referring to the inviolability of mail] should be removed. . . . Also, present restrictions on covert coverage should be relaxed on selective targets of priority foreign intelligence and internal security interest. . . . There is no valid argument against use of legal mail covers except Mr. Hoover's [J. Edgar Hoover, then Director of the Federal Bureau of Investigation] concern that the civil liberties people may become upset. This risk is surely an acceptable one and hardly serious enough to justify denying ourselves a valuable and legal intelligence tool. Covert coverage is illegal and there are serious risks involved. However, the advantages to be derived from its use outweigh the risks. This technique is particularly valuable in identifying espionage agents and other contacts of foreign intelligence services.

Huston went on to propound that techniques leading to what he called the "procurement of vitally needed foreign cryptographic material" should be modified. He informed the President that "use of this [newly proposed] technique is clearly illegal; it amounts to burglary. . . . It is also highly risky and would result in great embarrassment if exposed. However, it is also the most fruitful tool and can produce the type of intelligence which cannot be obtained in any other fashion."

And further: "Surreptitious entry of facilities occupied by subversive elements can turn up information about identities, methods of operation, and other invaluable investigative information which is not otherwise obtainable. This technique would be particularly helpful if used against the Weathermen and Black Panthers." Huston noted that "the deployment of the executive protective force has unfreezed [sic] the risk of surreptitious entry of diplomatic establishments. However, it is the belief of all except Mr. Hoover that the technique can still be successfully used on a selective basis."

What Huston was proposing, in effect, was that secret agents of the White House exert themselves to neutralize the protection of foreign diplomatic establishments in Washington, protection established by the Secret Service itself to assure the sanctity of foreign diplomatic missions on our soil. The Chilean Embassy in Washington was burglarized in May 1972, under circumstances that are still mysterious. (Chile then still had the elected Marxist regime of Salvador Allende Gossens, overthrown by the Chilean Army in September 1973.)

The whole intelligence plan was incredible. Small wonder that Senator Samuel J. Ervin, Jr., upon learning of it, described it as a "Gestapo" scheme certain to shock the American people.

How could Huston and the President's top advisers have conceived of such an approach to life in America? The question is enormously relevant to the whole Watergate situation, inasmuch as President Nixon approved the intelligence plan in a "decision memorandum" on July 5, 1970. The plan, in its final form a forty-three-page document, was prepared by the Interagency Committee on Intelligence, which warned the President that parts of it were "clearly illegal." On July 23, Nixon notified the four intelligence agencies (the CIA, the FBI, the National Security Agency, and the Defense Intelligence Agency) that the plan was to be implemented at once. He subsequently claimed that he had this order rescinded within five days, on July 28, but there is no record of such an action. In any event, the White House proceeded with a series of secret activities of its own, and in June 1971—eleven months later—created Hunt's Special Investigative Unit. Hunt and his associates then embarked on a series of operations that would have been plainly grotesque—Hunt in an ill-fitting red wig on secret missions and so on—if they hadn't resulted in crimes of political burglary and espionage committed under the authority of the President of the United States.

Hunt and his companions and hand-picked raiders were only one aspect of a much wider White House political enterprise, one evidently designed to keep Nixon in office for another term and to perpetuate in the American Presidency for an indefinite period an elite group of power brokers linked to powerful financial interests and determined to maintain the nation's social *status quo*. It may be pertinent to note here that Richard Nixon had always had a personal affinity for millionaires (this is illustrated by the roster of his closest friends), that a number of millionaires were employed in staff jobs at the White House, which is unusual in Presidential offices, and that the whole campaign-related operation was based on enormous covert expenditures of campaign money. Suffice it to say that in 1972 Nixon's campaign war chest exceeded $60 million, much of it collected through hard-sell solicitation bordering on extortion from big corporations. And, for what it is worth, Hunt himself had an obsession about making money, as much money as possible.

Senate investigators concluded in mid-1973 that from the day Nixon entered the White House in 1969, planning began for his second-term election. The widespread violence in the country in 1970, a part of the black and youth revolts and the revulsion against the Vietnam war, was used by the White House to rationalize its decision to create a "parallel" secret police, for which Howard Hunt was soon to be recruited by a top Presidential adviser. The Republicans' poor showing in the mid-term 1970 elections further persuaded the White House inner circle that extraordinary measures were urgently required to prevent a Democratic victory in 1972. This led to the programming of major covert political actions against the Democratic party. These were to include everything from planted smears and provocations to faked demonstrations and, in the end, "dirty tricks." And, of course, there were Hunt's political burglaries. While Hunt and his associates concentrated on White House–assigned intelligence work, a separate unit was set up in California by Donald H. Segretti, a young lawyer, to harass prominent candidates vying for the Democratic nomination. A plan was conceived to create a situation in which the Democrats would pick the weakest possible candidate—Nixon knew he could beat George S. McGovern but he was afraid of Edmund S. Muskie—to assure that a Nixon second term would win in a landslide in November. Nothing was forgotten. The leak of the Pentagon Papers was to be used to associate antiwar Democrats and the New Left with what a White House confidential memorandum called a "negative image" of virtual treason. An "enemy list" was developed at the White House. A memorandum written in August 1971 by John W. Dean III, counsel to the President, recommended that "the available Federal machinery" (by which he meant principally the Internal Revenue Service) be used to "screw our political enemies."

In an article entitled "The Aborted Nixon Revolution," Hans J. Morgenthau, the noted political scientist, wrote recently that Watergate in all its manifestations,

> has duplicated certain official, statutory investigative and law enforcement agencies with secret, unofficial ones, exempt from normal legal restraints; it has justified the disregard of constitutional and statutory restraints with concern for "national security," which in this context is a synonym for the "national emergency" by which fascism justified the destruction of the democratic order. Finally, its conservative pretenses have masked nihilistic destruction. . . . The perpetrators of Watergate have put their desire to hold on to power above observance of constitutional and statutory restraints. They have taken the first steps toward the transformation of American democracy in the image of authoritarian and totalitarian regimes where the struggle for power is carried on through the fraudulent use of democratic procedures, culminating in the suppression of dissent and the physical elimination of the dissenters. . . . [Hunt's squads] were called upon to perform in a haphazard way the same functions which the highly organized and disciplined secret police have traditionally performed in authoritarian and totalitarian societies.

What we see here, therefore, is an astonishing conflict between ethical concepts of right and wrong which, one always assumed, had been settled once and for all in a civilized society. Thus, we have Tom Huston, an unknown and inexperienced White House aide, offering to the President an intelligence plan that violated the Bill of Rights. We have the President of the United States accepting and then allegedly rescinding it. Huston had the candor to acknowledge that he was proposing illegal measures, but President Nixon has not satisfactorily addressed himself to this ethical issue. Up to mid-1970, one might have said that these were hypothetical situations and issues. But with Hunt and company on the scene the following year, things ceased to be hypothetical and became practical. Before a federal grand jury in

Washington in April 1973, on the subject of the raid he organized and supervised on the offices of Daniel Ellsberg's psychiatrist, he told the prosecutor, "I am not quibbling, but there's quite a difference between something that's legal and something that's clandestine. . . . I would simply call it an entry operation conducted under the auspices of competent authority." Later, before the Watergate Committee, he said he had been led to believe that the Special Unit worked under direct Presidential authority.

The raid on the psychiatrist's office by one of Hunt's Cuban-American teams was undertaken to get material about Ellsberg so that the CIA—in another domestic intelligence operation that is essentially unlawful for the Agency under the statute—could draw a "psychological profile" of the man who in the spring of 1971 had provided the American press with the Pentagon Papers detailing past military, intelligence, and diplomatic actions by the United States government in the Vietnam war. To the President and his closest assistants, Ellsberg's action constituted an act of treason. Ellsberg, though indicted for the Pentagon Papers, had not yet been tried, convicted, or sentenced. But the Hunt operators decided to take the law into their own hands.

Robert J. Myers, a former CIA official and now publisher of the liberal Washington weekly *The New Republic,* wrote in an article about Hunt (whom he knew slightly in the 1950s) that Hunt's ethics were, in effect, the product of his clandestine way of life.

This is the feeling of belonging, of being inside, that welds the CIA together. . . . It is the extra sanction to do what needs to be done that makes otherwise illegal acts legal. . . . One is reminded of Raskolnikov, the murderer in *Crime and Punishment,* rationalizing his axe slayings: ". . . whoever is strong in mind and spirit will have power over them. Anyone who is greatly daring is right in their eyes. He who despises most things will be a law-giver among them and he who dares most of all will be most in the right! So it has been till now and so it will always be." . . . The forces of good and evil are even for Raskolnikov at that point. For Hunt, they were always even if they had the CIA stamp.

What Myers had to say about Hunt and his CIA psychology goes also for the Nixon entourage, which evidently arrived at the same conclusions about power through their own experiences in the long practice of Nixon-brand politics. And the circle of White House ethics was closed when John D. Ehrlichman, the President's former chief domestic adviser, testified on July 27, 1973, before the Senate Select Committee on Watergate that the Ellsberg raid "was an effort on the part of the Special Unit to do, as they had done in other cases subsequently, to determine where there were holes in either the federal government itself or in the Rand Corporation [the think-tank funded by the government where Ellsberg had once worked] or these outside units that would permit a person like Ellsberg and his co-conspirators, if there were any, to steal massive quantities of top-secret documents and turn them over to the Russians." There is no proof, incidentally, that the Soviet Embassy actually received a set of the Pentagon Papers, although there are theories that the administration itself sent them to the Russians as a "provocation" while publication in the newspapers was held up pending the Supreme Court ruling.

I have cited these instances of how White House personnel interpreted the Constitution and the traditional ethical concepts in order to establish the psychological—if not psychotic—frame of mind in which all this was developing, unbeknown to the American people.

As I said earlier, President Nixon's philosophy does not concern me in this particular context. And presumably one could explain Tom Huston's intelligence plan as an aberration by a young man prematurely drawn into a situation of extraordinary power associated with White House tenure. One could even set aside Ehrlichman's *post facto* rationalization of the burglaries, inasmuch as he appeared before the Senate Committee as a defender of the President and an advocate of his ideas. Both Huston and Ehrlichman had had only a shallow exposure to the world of modern politics, and no real sense of what constitutes foreign or domestic intelligence operations—only an instinct that they would be politically useful.

Howard Hunt, however, is another story. He is the product of the shadowy world of international intelligence, a fanatical Cold War fighter, and a man whose entire adult and professional experience was related to the craft of subversion. First in the Office of Strategic Service, fighting the Japanese in World War II, and subsequently in the CIA, where he battled the heresy of communism with religious fervor, Hunt emerges as a personality whose life encompasses all the travails of a clandestine agent who operates against any target assigned to him by "proper authorities." In this sense, then, Hunt's road to Watergate began in the jungles of Burma and China, led through postwar intrigues in Paris, Vienna, and Tokyo, and through Latin American conspiracies—ranging from the ouster of a leftist Guatemalan president to the aborted invasion of Cuba at the Bay of Pigs, not to mention other assorted acts of intelligence-craft mischief.

We also know that Hunt lived a life in which reality and fantasy often overlapped. His penchant for producing spy novels in prodigious numbers—he wrote forty-five of them over the years—seemed to reveal how the line between reality and a dream world became progressively blurred in his mind. As a former CIA superior of his remarked to me not long ago, "Howard was always play-acting, really acting out a fantasy rather than functioning in a reasonably rational fashion."

All of this makes Howard Hunt a very interesting, indeed strangely fascinating, human being. But, at this point, we must ask ourselves two questions: what was it in his pre-Watergate life that fashioned him into the kind of man he is? And how could the highest officials of this Republic have possibly turned to him to execute *at home* operations that normally fitted into international espionage and to act out *at home* his manifold fantasies?

Since Watergate, Howard Hunt has been beset by tragedy. His wife died in a plane crash in Chicago not quite six months after the 1972 Watergate break-in. Hunt himself was provisionally sentenced to thirty-five years in prison. He left behind four teen-age children, one of whom has serious medical problems. He has been beaten in jail by fellow inmates and, in mid-1973, apparently suffered a minor stroke. Yet Hunt, despite his oft-proclaimed and single-minded devotion to what he perceives as duty to his country and his President, became in the words of his White House employers a "blackmailer" for money after he was imprisoned, threatening to reveal the "dirty tricks" he had performed for the President's staff if the money were not paid. He received the money, but this was in vain. He and many others testified before a grand jury and before Congressional committees, and his story and that of Watergate unfolded before the nation.

Howard Hunt, then, is a tragic, tortured, and frustrated figure. To understand his many, often contradictory obsessions and to gain insight into the psychology and the mentality which spawned men like him, it is necessary to retrace his steps over the long span of years and to survey the road that led him from the jungles of Southeast Asia to the burglary of the Watergate.

To try to understand Howard Hunt, we must take a quick glance at the history of the last quarter of a century, at the Cold War, at the clash of ideologies, and at the very special kind of existence that a professional undercover CIA agent lives. We know that Hunt was a somewhat compulsive clandestine operator, but we need to examine the world in which he matured into the kind of man he is. I do not want to suggest that *all* former and present CIA officials, case officers, and agents are replicas of Howard Hunt. A great many of them have emerged unscathed from the great intelligence wars. Hunt and others, quite clearly, did not.

Howard Hunt's career paralleled the life of the CIA almost from its inception. The agency was created in July 1947 under the National Security Act signed by President Harry S. Truman, to bring under one roof all the intelligence-gathering facilities of the United States government. Prior to that time, the United States lacked a centralized intelligence organization—lagging far behind Britain, the Soviet Union, Germany, Japan, France, and many other smaller nations. When World War II broke out, American intelligence activities were concentrated largely in the civilian hands of the Federal Bureau of Investigation and in military intelligence—the G-2 section of the United States Army and the Office of Naval Intelligence. But none of this equipped the United States with an adequate capability for collecting intelligence, conducting effective wartime espionage, or engaging in the clandestine missions which, increasingly, were playing a key role in the conduct of the war. After Pearl Harbor, where the United States was partly the victim of an intelligence failure, President Roosevelt, realizing this weakness, picked William J. Donovan, a New York lawyer, to lay the foundations for a modern and comprehensive intelligence organization. Donovan started out with a small office, known at first as the COI (Coordinator of Information), soon transformed and expanded into the now famous OSS (Office of Strategic Services), with a mandate "to collect and analyze strategic information and to plan and operate special services."

The OSS, though lacking the great traditions of the British

Intelligence Service, performed brilliantly during the war in both Asia and Europe. It was staffed by some of the brightest, best-born, and best-educated young people of their generation. Howard Hunt, then twenty-five years old but not truly part of this American patrician elite, was an OSS operative in the Chinese theater. As a friend of his was to remark many years later, "This was when Howard was bitten by the bug of intelligence and espionage and that's when he flipped." As subsequent events were to show, he never quite recovered from his first exhilarating experience.

With the advent of peace, the OSS was no longer in a position to meet the needs imposed by the postwar period, the eruption of the Cold War, and the rapidly changing requirements of intelligence, which already at that time was more and more dependent on technology. The romantic period had come to its end—or, at least, should have come to its end when the OSS was disbanded. The realization in the government that a professional and multifaceted intelligence organization was now needed led to the creation of the CIA's forerunner, the Central Intelligence Group, which essentially was a hodgepodge of wartime intelligence and espionage operators. But the group had no clear mandate, did not fit rationally into the structure of the government, and nobody quite seemed to know what were its functions and responsibilities. Nor, for that matter, did anyone really know who was in charge of it in terms of the over-all foreign policies of the United States.

So the CIA was created to function as a modern agency with, it was hoped, reasonably well-defined lines of responsibility. It is one of the peculiarities of the American political system that we tend to confuse the public and secret images of organizations that we set in motion. The United States is, I believe, one of the few, if not the only, modern nation to have established an intelligence agency, by definition a secret enterprise, through the passage of a public act of the legislature. To proclaim publicly the establishment of an intelligence agency is an act of faith proper in an open society, which the United States has always prided itself to be. But commendable as such an approach may be, in intelligence work a basic contradiction immediately develops. To be effective, an intelligence agency has to work in secrecy. The advantage to Americans and to the world of being aware of the CIA's existence is, therefore, quickly dissipated by the very secrecy under which it must work and live.

The 1947 legislation described in general terms the mandate of the CIA in such obvious fields as the collection and analysis of intelligence, and the supply of intelligence estimates to policymakers. Beyond this vague mandate, extraordinary power and authority were vested both in the Agency and in the government of which it is a part. Allen W. Dulles, the most famous of CIA directors and the man who headed it during the immensely controversial years between 1953 and 1961, remarked in his book *The Craft of Intelligence* that the CIA "has, of course, a secret side and the law permits the National Security Council which, in effect, means the President, to assign to the CIA certain duties and functions in the intelligence field in addition to those specifically enumerated in the law. These functions are not disclosed."

In a sense, then, it can be argued—and it has been argued—that nobody truly controls the CIA. Its annual budget in the 1970s is estimated somewhere around $6 billion, and a good guess is that it employs around ten thousand persons. Appropriations to the CIA are never disclosed and, instead, are buried by the Bureau of the Budget in the budgets of other government agencies. To comply with the law, several Congressional committees and subcommittees theoretically have an overseeing function over the CIA, but for the last quarter of a century Senators and Representatives on these panels have asked little and learned less about what the Agency is thinking or doing.

Under the system in existence since the Eisenhower Presidency, a special committee of the National Security Council—known in the 1970s as the 40 Committee—is charged with the power of instructing the CIA and the rest of the sprawling intelligence community as to how and where to proceed. But what remains unclear to this day is the precise extent to which the 40 Committee, the full National Security Council, or the President of the United States specifically assigns tasks to the intelligence agencies or simply sets forth broad policies—or targets—under which they are free to perform according to their lights.

The 40 Committee's deliberations are, of course, top secret, and even its existence is not publicly discussed by the administration. (The group's present name, incidentally, is derived from the number of the National Security Council memorandum which reorganized it in 1969.) It is chaired by Henry A. Kissinger, the President's Secretary of State and Special Assistant for National Security Affairs, and it includes the heads of the CIA (the CIA Director also acts in his capacity as Director of Central Intelligence coordinating *all* governmental intelligence activities), the Defense Intelligence Agency, and the National Security Agency; the Deputy Secretary of State; and the Deputy Secretary of Defense. The 40 Committee has the power to make decisions in every field, although they are subject to Presidential veto. But only the President is empowered to order the intelligence community to commit acts of political assassination in a foreign country. There is no record, naturally, of such an act ever being ordered by the President of the United States, but intelligence-community insiders say it has happened on a few occasions. Neither the 40 Committee nor the President concern themselves with garden-variety murders in the wars of intelligence agents. These occur on all sides with a certain frequency, but they come to public attention only by accident. A clandestine CIA (or KGB) agent knows that violent death is a risk of his métier. Sometimes, knowledgeable CIA people claim, on a particularly sensitive assignment the Agency can totally bypass the 40 Committee by using the simple expedient of temporarily assigning an American agent to a friendly foreign intelligence service, such as the British MI-6, to perform his task theoretically under other auspices than the CIA's. Under existing agreements with several British Commonwealth, West German, and other governments, foreign agents may conversely operate out of the CIA.

The history of the last twenty-five years has demonstrated the ease with which the CIA may find itself drawn into operations that have turned into disaster and brought acute embarrassment to the United States. Other operations have been successful on the surface, but nevertheless highly controversial. But the CIA's view is that some of its most successful undertakings in the national interest must remain unknown to the public. This may well be right, but the end result is that the CIA over the years has been singled out as a villain committing intelligence operations that have failed or aroused controversy at home and abroad, while its other enterprises, quite possibly constructive and positive, have gone unsung.

Often, it is a matter of professional and political judgment which operations do make sense and which do not. It can be argued that in the kind of world we live in today, the CIA's U-2 high-altitude flights over the Soviet Union and China were a necessary defensive part of our intelligence operations before new technology allowed development of the SAMOS orbiting satellites. The United States needed to know all it could about Soviet missile deployment and other military activities. But the U-2 became a symbol of failure when one was shot down over the Soviet Union in 1960. Very few people, even in the Agency, will argue that the Bay of Pigs invasion of Cuba made much sense in either its inception or execution. There are divided opinions about the wisdom of the CIA's covert Congo operations during the 1960s. The dominant view is that the CIA acquitted itself well in 1953 when it ousted Iran's nationalistic premier, Mohammed Mossadegh, and restored to the throne the Shah—to this day a devoted ally. And to some Americans, the overthrow of the Guatemalan government of President Jacobo Arbenz Guzman in 1954 was an undertaking fully in tune with the proper defense of the Western Hemisphere against alleged Communist penetration. To others, it was a brazen intervention in the affairs of a small nation. The CIA is also responsible for one of our most fundamental disasters in Southeast Asia—the demolition of a coalition government in Laos in 1960—and it is at best debatable whether it acted wisely or even helpfully when it involved itself in the mid-1960s and later in building a secret army of Meo tribesmen in Laos in the context of the widening Indochina war. One could go on forever discussing the pros and cons of individual CIA operations. But what continues to be disturbing, considering the kind of society we are, or like to think we are, is that one is never quite sure what the next brainstorm in the intelligence community will be and what the likely results will be. In 1973, in the Watergate hearings and investigations, the quite proper question was raised as to the degree of the CIA's participation in domestic intelligence plans or operations. By law it is supposed to have none. Yet the White House intelligence plan, that extraordinary document drafted by Tom Huston, assigned to the CIA a specific role in domestic intelligence in violation of its statute. And even after these disclosures, no senior official of the CIA has been prepared to pledge the Agency publicly to a policy of noninvolvement in domestic affairs, even though the law clearly proscribes such activities. Testimony in the Watergate hearings made the point that to at least some degree the CIA, on White House orders or otherwise, provided support functions for the President's secret Special Investigative Unit and, specifically, for its alumnus Howard Hunt.

It is easy, of course, to speak from hindsight. But there has been foresight, too, and it went unheeded. In February 1947, five months before the CIA became operative, George C. Marshall, then Secretary of State, warned President Truman that the plans for the new agency were questionable because "its

powers . . . seemed almost unlimited and need clarification."
General Marshall, probably one of the wisest men to serve American Presidents in postwar years, may have had in mind the language of the law which provided that the CIA had authority to
"perform for the benefit of existing intelligence agencies such
additional services of common concern as the National Security
Council determines can be more effectively accomplished cen-
trally." Another potentially dangerous provision in the law allowed
the Agency to "perform such other functions and duties related
to intelligence affecting the national security as the National
Security Council may from time to time direct." General Marshall
could not have anticipated how dramatically right he would be
proven in the years to come. He may not have even given thought
to the psychology and philosophy that was bound to develop in
an organization of such unlimited powers which does not appear
to be fully accountable to anybody. And he may have overlooked
what such power will do to men—individuals like E. Howard
Hunt, Jr., and others.

There is no easy explanation of what makes a man become an
intelligence agent or a spy. But Allen Dulles himself tells us
something important about the men who go into clandestine intelligence services when he quotes in *The Craft of Intelligence* the
characterization of the spy Caypor in an old story by Somerset
Maugham. Here is Maugham's description: "It might be he was
one of those men who preferred devious ways to straight for some
intricate pleasure they get in fooling their fellows . . . that he

had turned spy . . . from a desire to score off the big-wigs who never even knew of his existence. It might be that it was vanity that had impelled him, a feeling that his talents had not received the recognition they merited, or just a puckish, impish desire to do mischief."

In some ways, this well describes Howard Hunt's personality traits. But the most curious of all is that Hunt himself quietly collaborated with Dulles in drafting the former CIA Director's book, although the Agency nowadays denies this with vigor. It is logical and not so surprising that this passage would have caught the attention of Hunt, a compulsive author of spy novels. So often frustrated by the sense that his own talents were not justly rewarded, a feeling expressed throughout his novels and his conversations with friends, Hunt might have recognized himself in Maugham's psychological profile of the spy Caypor.

When the CIA was created in 1947—Howard Hunt joined it a year or so later—the United States and the Soviet Union were confronting each other in the opening years of the Cold War. Barely two years had passed since the defeat of Nazi Germany by American, British, and Soviet forces, but now the lines in the ideological and political conflict between the East and the West were clearly drawn. It is not relevant for the purposes of this account to make judgments as to which side was responsible for the Cold War, or to enter into the arguments of recent years as to whether the Soviet Union or the United States is to blame for the Cold War. Historically, there is no question that the Soviet Union under Stalin was engaged in consolidating postwar power in Eastern Europe and, ideologically, imposing Communist regimes in East European countries. Whether Stalin planned not only to consolidate his wartime gains but also to expand Soviet influence all over Europe, Asia, and the world is a question of historical analysis. But there is clear evidence nonetheless that the Kremlin had political and ideological plans that went beyond the establishment of a defensive belt in Eastern

Europe. There were, for example, Soviet efforts to encourage pro-Communist rebellions in Greece. (This was before Marshal Tito split away from the Communist monolith, and Yugoslavia at that time still served as an operational base for Greek rebels.) In 1948, Moscow engineered a *coup d'état* in Czechoslovakia which ended three years of Czech democracy and established a hard-line Communist regime. Then there were efforts to take over Azerbaijan, in northern Iran, in the Soviets' first move into the oil-rich Middle East. Whether or not Stalin might have been talked out of this forward pattern by Anglo-American negotiators remains a moot point.

What is relevant, however, is that the West, notably the United States, perceived Soviet policy as a major threat to its own interests as well as to allied countries in Western Europe and the Middle East. The United States, rightly or wrongly, convinced itself that it faced a world-wide Communist menace, and American policies under President Truman and Dean Acheson, his Secretary of State, began to be fashioned accordingly.

The Cold War was officially declared, so to speak, by the United States in 1947, with the proclamation of the Truman Doctrine of aiding Greece and Turkey against Communist pressures, and with the launching of the Marshall Plan in May to provide massive aid to America's Western allies so that their war-shattered economies could be reconstructed and the dangers of internal Communist takeovers thereby diffused. One must remember that the French and Italian Communist parties were then at the apex of their power, and the United States government saw itself faced not only by what it regarded as Stalin's direct aggressive designs, but also by Communist-guided internal subversion in Western Europe. Had it not been for massive American assistance in every field, the Communists might have defeated the Christian Democrats in Italy's 1948 general elections. On March 12, 1947, President Truman told Congress that the security of the United States was threatened by communism and that it would be American policy "to help free peoples to maintain their free institutions and their national integrity against aggressive movements seeking to impose on them totalitarian regimes." The United States, he said, would not stand still for Communist "coercion or . . . such subterfuges as political infiltration."

In his book, Allen Dulles related this political perception to the needs of American intelligence. The United States was "witnessing the first stages of a master plan to shatter the societies of Europe and Asia and isolate the United States, and eventually to take over the entire world," he wrote. At that time, "we were coming to realize . . . the need to learn a great deal more than we knew about the secret plans of the Kremlin to advance the frontiers of Communism." This was the general state of mind in Washington when the CIA was established in early 1947. Inevitably, the new agency's mission reflected the concerns of the American leadership, as expressed by Truman and later by Allen Dulles.

The CIA's primary and overwhelming role was to act as a defensive-offensive weapon against world-wide communism. It was in this spirit that the Agency began functioning under its first Director, Roscoe Henry Hillenkoetter, an admiral with a background in Naval Intelligence. The recruits for the new agency came in the first instance from the OSS, men who had learned the craft of clandestine operation under wartime conditions, and from the ranks of Army and Navy intelligence specialists. Quickly, however, the CIA also began attracting personnel from among well-educated Ivy League graduates, well-born young people who might have otherwise moved into big business and Wall Street, as well as from groups of individuals with diplomatic and consular State Department experience. Specialists were needed, too. The Agency turned on one level to intellectuals and scholars in an extraordinary variety of fields. On another level, it went after agents and "nuts-and-bolts" security specialists

—people who knew how to forge passports and identity papers, establish secret listening and transmission devices (we were then in the infancy of that electronic art which blossomed forth at Watergate a quarter of a century later), develop invisible writing and coding and decoding of secret messages, provide experts with personal weapons—in short, the technical-support branch of the Agency. The CIA set up special intelligence schools, including the famous "Farm" in the Maryland countryside.

As is the case with most new organizations, it was intended that the CIA would be the most perfect in its field. Its founders had in mind a highly coordinated intelligence operation in which all clandestine work in the United States government would be under one roof. As Allen Dulles was to remark later, there would be no compartmentalization, "which so often leads to neither the right hand nor the left knowing what the other is doing," but a perfect synchronization between the CIA's operational and analytical divisions. Presumably, the Agency's Director and his immediate senior staff were to coordinate these activities. But what looked good on paper did not necessarily happen in practice. As it developed, not only did other top officials in the government not know what the CIA was doing here or there, but almost as often one side of the Agency was in the dark about the thoughts and activities of the other. Whether the CIA Director is really in a position to ride herd on the entire Agency is a point that still eludes intelligence specialists. The CIA was reorganized several times, most recently in 1973, to deal with these problems. As the Agency grew over the years into a monster organization —with some ten thousand employees at the Washington headquarters and an unknown number of agents, employees, informants, and tipsters in virtually every corner of the world —bureaucratic law inevitably prevailed. The great cohesive intelligence outfit was turning into a many-headed animal. In time, sharp clashes developed between the thoughtful analysts and political interpreters in the Directorate of Current Intelligence and the clandestine activists in the Directorate of Plans. These conflicts between the Current Intelligence division and the clandestine services brought about many disasters. Often, the clandestine people, who frequently sought support for their cause in other power centers within the government, ignored the analysts. This pattern was to plague the American intelligence community all the way up to the end of the Vietnam war.

Another pitfall for the new agency was whether it could in fact stay away from policy-making or, at least, policy-influencing in the government. Allen Dulles wrote in 1963—obviously with hindsight—that the CIA initially was supposed to be excluded from policy-making and would avoid "to the greatest possible extent the bending of fact obtained through i   ence to suit a particular occupational viewpoint."

I don't know whether Dulles   eved this as late as 1963, or whether he was coverin   tionalizing situations in which the CIA had overtly or   ayed a role in fashioning policies to suit its own view   ed interests. But one should not forget that for nearl   s, while Allen Dulles was head of the CIA, his brother   oster Dulles, was Secretary of State. It was clear at the out   that the two brothers did see eye to eye on many things. On the basis of common sense and from what is now known about this brother act, it can safely be concluded that through Allen Dulles the intelligence community had a powerful voice in Presidential decision-making.

Allen Dulles made no secret of this close personal and political relationship with his brother. In his book, he describes this "precious association" when Foster became Secretary of State in 1953 and "I was promoted from my job of Deputy, in which I had served under President Truman, to that of Director of Central Intelligence."

Foster early saw grave new dangers to peace in the philosophy and policies of Communism. He became a convinced supporter of the work of the new Central Intelligence Agency. He wanted to check his own impressions and those of his associates in the State Department against an outside factual analysis of the problems which the President and he were facing. . . . He sought the testing of his views against the hard realities of intelligence appraisals which marshaled the elements of each crisis situation. It was the duty of intelligence to furnish just this to the President and the Secretary of State.

But things tended to work out differently in many day-to-day situations. John Foster Dulles approached the world and foreign policy with a quasi-mystical attitude. To him, communism always was "atheistic," and neutralism was a dirty word. The two brothers shared this dogmatic and uncompromising view of the world, and they were neither open-minded nor truly willing to test their views against the "hard realities of intelligence appraisals" if these ran counter to their preconceptions. Hard-line anticommunism was the officially sanctioned policy in the Agency, and dissenters were brought up short. Convinced right-wingers—Howard Hunt is the best case in point—were, on the other hand, in favor with the CIA's Executive Office.

An important example of this state of affairs was that in 1954 the best CIA analysts began to see, long before the rest of Washington came to grips with this reality, that communism was no longer monolithic and that a split was quietly developing between the Soviet Union and China. Shortly before Secretary Dulles went to Geneva to attend the 1954 conference, marking the end of the French war in Indochina, a series of position papers were prepared in the Directorate of Current Intelligence suggesting that such a split might be in the making, and that the Secretary might be well advised to take advantage of it and establish some sort of relationship with Chou En-lai, the Chinese premier, who was also going to attend the Geneva meeting. Allen Dulles transmitted these studies (with no recommendations of his own) to his brother. Secretary Dulles, in turn, relayed it to his Far Eastern expert, Walter S. Robertson, a firm supporter of the Nationalist Chinese and a total believer that communism must, indeed, be monolithic. Robertson's conclusion was that the CIA analysts were in effect out of their minds. Secretary Dulles passed this advice back to his brother, who instantly instructed his Current Intelligence people to stop coming up with nonsensical papers and ideas. Shortly thereafter, Dulles was in Geneva, refusing even to shake the proffered hand of Chou En-lai.

Many years later the CIA's clandestine division militants sold Allen Dulles on the disastrous idea of mounting an invasion of Cuba at the Bay of Pigs. Dulles in turn sold it to President Eisenhower and Vice President Nixon. And in the previous year, 1960, the CIA had distinguished itself by a series of political acts in Laos which led to the aggravation of the entire Indochina situation. Although, so far as it is known, no specific instructions to that effect were issued by President Eisenhower, the CIA's clandestine operators took it upon themselves to undermine the coalition government in Laos because in their obsessive anti-communism they could not tolerate the neutralist premier, Souvanna Phouma. The Agency's next major contribution to the welfare of Laos was the establishment of its own secret army based on the Meo tribesmen, often mercenaries.

Ironically, though, the CIA was more often right than wrong in the Vietnam war. Thus, in 1969, when President Nixon took office, CIA analysts strongly discouraged the notion, dearly held by the military, that heavy bombings of North Vietnam—such as those carried out during the Johnson administration prior to the 1968 agreement, which produced the Paris negotiations and the bombing halt—would not bring Hanoi to its knees. Nixon, of course, did not heed this advice. But they continued to urge caution and realism. Sitting in their cubicles in Langley, Virginia, they had no vested interests, unlike the agents in the field. In fact, they made themselves highly unpopular with many key people in the Nixon administration because of their insistence that the Pentagon was wildly exaggerating "kill ratios" among the North Vietnamese and the Viet Cong and otherwise distorting the battlefield situation, presumably because it made the armed forces look good. Classified studies prepared in the CIA also suggested the inconsistencies in the military position. How, the analysts asked, could the Saigon command claim this heavy destruction of the enemy forces and at the same time keep asking for more and more troops and war materiel from the United States in order to win the war?

But the Agency's clandestine people in Indochina had other ideas than the analysts in Langley. In Vietnam, the CIA was deeply involved in projects such as Operation Phoenix, a program designed to eradicate the Viet Cong infrastructure. Working with the Vietnamese National Police, the CIA helped to organize assassination squads, each of which had a quota for captured and killed Viet Cong agents. In a perverse sort of way, the CIA planners of Operation Phoenix were goaded into action by the opinion of the analysts at home—and a correct one it was—that the Communist infrastructure cadres were increasing rather than diminishing. At the same time, the enormous CIA operation in Saigon had a vested interest, based on Parkinson's Law, in expanding its power and influence. Likewise, the CIA, working from South Vietnam and Thailand, participated in secret incursions made by U. S. Special Forces into Cambodia as early as 1969, when President Nixon was still proclaiming our neutrality in that country. Throughout this time, the CIA station chief in Saigon (William E. Colby, named the CIA's Director in mid-1973, was one of them) operated on the same level as the U. S. Ambassador and the top military commander.

What had been planned as a coherent intelligence agency became a fractionalized one in which disagreements were rampant and where the right hand seldom knew what the left was doing. But whatever the CIA's internal and external disputes, the overriding fact was that it continued to operate on the basis of an unrelenting anticommunism. The CIA's first concern, of course, was the Soviet Union, with China not too far behind. As Allen Dulles wrote:

In the Soviet Union we are faced with an antagonist who has raised the art of espionage to an unprecedented height, while developing the collateral techniques of subversion and deception into a formidable political instrument of attack. No other country has ever before attempted this on such a scale. These operations, in support of the USSR's over-all policies, go on in times of so-called thaw and under the guise of coexistence with the same vigor as in times of actual crises. Our intelligence has a major share of the task of neutralizing such hostile activities, which present a common danger to us and our allies.

Nobody in his right mind will quarrel with the concept that there is such a thing as Soviet espionage and subversive operations and that they are highly "saturated," if not always of the best quality. It certainly was true during the formative years of the CIA; it remained so during the 1950s and well into the 1960s. It would be foolish to assume that because of the détente of the 1970s the Soviet KGB has gone out of business and that it now dedicates itself to pastoral callings. But today the art of espionage and subversion has become more sophisticated, and there is increasing reliance on technology and less on "dirty tricks" and the men so adept at them.

In the late 1940s, however, when Howard Hunt and so many other OSS veterans joined the new Agency, they faced an old-fashioned intelligence war of astounding proportions between the United States and the Soviet Union. It was in this war that the personalities and the character of CIA men were molded. This was the ambience in which Hunt lived, and it marked him for life.

As I remarked earlier, the CIA recruitment for high-level posts and even down to the ranks of case officers was from the educated American elite. The Agency was definitely an elitist organization. And the curious thing about the CIA men was that many of them were not classical right-wing or conservative types, but, instead, liberals of old tradition. However, as we have learned, American liberals become hawkish when they are in positions of power. As a matter of fact, they were political idealists in the practice of the craft of intelligence.

Picking names at random, there was, of course, first of all Allen Dulles himself, member of a famous American family who spent a lifetime in espionage—during World War I he was the agent in Switzerland who just missed meeting Lenin—and interspersed his wartime intelligence activities with the practice of law in the Eastern Establishment. There was Kermit Roosevelt, a grandson of President Theodore Roosevelt, who became after his OSS period a very sophisticated and often effective intelligence officer. (Roosevelt's dealings with Egypt's President Gamal Abdel Nasser in the 1950s might have redounded to considerable benefit to American interests had not the White House and the State Department held other ideas on how to deal with Arabs.) Richard McG. Helms, the Agency's Director until early 1973, was educated in an exclusive school in Switzerland, and, as a young newspaperman, he scored with an exclusive interview with Hitler shortly before the war. He spent his postwar years in the "black"—clandestine—side of the Agency before rising to be a Deputy Director and finally boss of the American intelligence establishment.

The list of brilliant men who served—or still serve—in the CIA is very long indeed. There is Richard M. Bissell, the economist who helped to put together the Marshall Plan and later became a CIA black operator and the man directly responsible for the U-2 program and, less felicitously, for the Bay of Pigs. Kenneth T. Downs, now head of a public-relations firm in New York and Washington, worked with Roosevelt in the Middle East. The conservative columnist William F. Buckley, Jr., and the liberal columnist Thomas W. Braden are both CIA alumni. So are the publishers of *The New Republic* and the *Washingtonian* magazines. Robert Amory, Jr., currently general counsel for the National Gallery of Art, is a former Deputy Director of the CIA. Another senior Agency official became after his retirement the treasurer for Eugene J. McCarthy's presidential campaign in 1968 and is now a fund-raiser for the Democratic party.

The armed forces, too, have provided their share of manpower for the intelligence community, in addition to their involvement in the Pentagon's own intelligence services. General Robert E. Cushman, Jr., presently Commandant of the Marine Corps, was attached to the CIA in the 1950s as a colonel (sharing an office with Howard Hunt) and later returned to be a Deputy Director in 1971, at a time when Hunt and his operatives were seeking CIA support for their secret White House operations. General Walter Bedell Smith, once Army Chief of Staff, was the CIA's second Director. (The law, incidentally, provides that if a civilian is CIA Director, his top deputy must be a military officer —and vice versa.)

The men I have mentioned—and many others—are well known and have eventually become well adjusted to normal civilian life after leaving the CIA. Others, however, have not so adjusted, have failed to make the transition to normalcy. Therein lies the story of compulsive agents like Howard Hunt.

If we accept the premise that well-educated and reasonably liberal men, in the best sense of the term, became fervent anti-Communists during the Cold War years in the name of what they then perceived as the defense of democratic ideals and principles, then it is small wonder that so many others, sometimes of different backgrounds, found it difficult to shift away from this attitude, and from the clandestine work they once were called upon to perform for their country. These intelligence men regarded themselves as dedicated patriots to whom performing missions for the United States and against communism was the best contribution they could make in public service. At the same time, they had to be individuals with a special bent for romantic adventure. Both in Howard Hunt's spy novels, and in real life, CIA men saw themselves as an elite. American writers have not yet produced a James Bond of their own (unless one regards Upton Sinclair's Lanny Budd as a forerunner of this kind of man). Terry and the Pirates and later Steve Canyon were, on the comic pages of newspapers, the closest version of the invincible intelligence operative. Only since Watergate made Howard Hunt a name familiar to millions of Americans, have we discovered that in his dozens of novels he has drawn a composite picture of the American intelligence agent. Unlike James Bond, the composite hero of Hunt's books is not always the winner in his contests with the forces of evil—as in real life the CIA agent may sometimes be defeated—and in this fashion Hunt in his own way is more honest and realistic than Ian Fleming. But, then, Hunt had lived the life of the undercover agent and he was sensitive enough to transpose to the pages of his books the truth that the craft of intelligence is both a winning and a losing game.

I asked a retired senior CIA man whether he considered Hunt—as we now know him through the inverted telescope lens of the Watergate affair—as a typical Agency officer or as an aberration. My companion thought this over. Unfortunately, "Howard was all too typical." I asked him to elaborate.

"You must understand," he said, "that in the great intelligence wars such agents thought of themselves as front-line soldiers. They were trained to be hard and resilient—and, if possible, emotionless—but humans are humans and they must respond accordingly, no matter how they might have been preconditioned. People, you see, die in intelligence work. And their companions, even their close friends, take it personally. Let me give you an example. At some point in the 1950s, we were secretly supporting an anti-Soviet independence movement among Ukrainians in West Germany. Among them there was a rather exceptional operator who worked closely with the CIA. One day, in Munich, while riding down an escalator he was murdered by someone who obviously was a Soviet agent. The assassination was done with the sting of a poison needle. Death was instantaneous. A CIA man who was the Ukrainian's control officer was a few steps away when it happened. To him this was an episode he will never forget. He became tougher and harder and more anti-Communist. And there have been scores and scores of such incidents. They all form part of the secret legend of the CIA—in the sense of terribly painful things seen and remembered." Two of Howard Hunt's close CIA friends—Rutherford J. Walsh (known as "Pinkie" and once station chief in Syria) and Glenn Morehouse—died mysteriously in recent years.

Intelligence work is very demanding, and it often drives men to points of unbearable tension. A senior CIA official of my acquaintance spent a "lost weekend" with a succession of bottles of Scotch because it had been his lot to order an assassination somewhere. And there have been many cases, seldom publicized, of suicide among intelligence officials.

All these pressures converge most strongly on the anonymous secret operative. Years of secret existence in several different countries under a variety of covers inevitably affect his personality. He gains a special sense of power as well as a special sense of detachment from normal life. Where such an agent might have started in his professional life with a sense of pragmatism, after a while he tends to become wedded to the single-minded pursuit of his professional activities, and to an equally single-minded ideological position. Usually, there is no room for intellectual or political compromise. An enormous sense of loyalty develops within this elite corps, and this also leads to an unquestioning acceptance of orders from above. Innumerable CIA agents I have known consider themselves in many ways above the laws written for mere mortals. It is not altogether illogical for a man like Hunt to believe honestly that his acts in the Watergate period were perfectly acceptable because they were conducted under the auspices of what he called "proper authority." Reading his secret testimony before a federal grand jury, I had the impression that Hunt was somewhat bewildered that *other* proper authorities, such as the grand jury, might be questioning the correctness of his acts. After all, had he not been acting on the authority of the President of the United States or men directly under his command?

The CIA *esprit de corps* is so strong among many present and past CIA men that some of them, too, are confused as to why Hunt has been criticized, convicted, and sentenced. The more senior people—the CIA patricians—take the view that Hunt had flipped and that he had acted criminally. Hunt was never held in high esteem by these men, to put it mildly. But others see him as a victim of an ungrateful establishment. In August 1973, shortly after a magazine in New York published an article I wrote that was rather critical of Howard Hunt, I had occasion to lunch with James W. McCord, Jr., one of the convicted Watergate raiders who had operated under Hunt's orders. He was out on bail, having in effect turned state's evidence. McCord, an ex-CIA employee, was an extraordinary study in psychological contrasts. It was because of his letter to a Washington judge in March 1973 that the whole Watergate case was reopened, following the January trial at which all those implicated had either pleaded or been found guilty and had maintained their vows of silence. McCord decided to break this silence after being subjected to intense pressure to accept a cover story, apparently advocated by the White House, that the CIA was responsible for Watergate. He had spent nineteen years as a security specialist with the CIA, and was so totally faithful to it that he chose to tell all that he knew about Watergate—thereby setting in motion a political process of colossal proportions—rather than permit his beloved Agency to be besmirched. Hunt was among those who not only had agreed to go for the CIA cover-up story but personally pressed McCord to go along with it. Yet McCord in his own way still remained loyal even to Hunt. When I asked him during lunch to talk to me about Hunt, he told me in his soft voice that in writing critically about Hunt I had performed a signal "disservice to your country," and that he simply would not converse with me about the man who was the direct cause of so many of his troubles. What prompted Hunt, in contrast, to turn to blackmail and agree to participate in an effort to discredit the CIA is a part of the story I shall come to later.

What usually happens to men who resign or retire from the CIA? How is society affected by the men who rejoin its ranks after long years of clandestinity and a very special attitude toward the exercise of power and the laws governing their fellow citizens?

There are, naturally, several answers, and they vary according to the personalities and backgrounds of the individuals involved. One factor that is present is what one might call the elitist factor. At the top of the scale, there are well-connected men who make an easy transition to prestigious jobs and positions. In their CIA days they never lose contact with the Eastern Establishment, and their financial, family, Ivy League, and social links remain intact. They form something of a close fraternity within the ranks of former CIA people, with friendships dating back in some cases to OSS days. There is something almost British about them. Washington boasts quite a few of these figures, and they are very much part of the Georgetown social set. As the saying goes, they are acceptable and accepted. They do not hide their CIA past and, in fact, enjoy chatting about it with friends and acquaintances, though they respect the pledge of secrecy all CIA employees must take upon leaving the Agency concerning their specific activities in intelligence work.

There is another group about which there is virtually no public awareness. These are the men who have shifted from intelligence work in the CIA to intelligence activities in the private sector. Although this is not widely known, an increasing number of big corporations in recent years have either established private intelligence units or hired intelligence consultants from the CIA, the FBI, the DIA, the Internal Security Division of the Justice Department, the Treasury, the Secret Service, or the Internal Revenue Service. The purpose is, basically, to protect a corporation's own secrets or acquire other corporations' secrets in the ever-competitive business world. A whole underworld of corporate intelligence has thus developed.

Several organizations in the United States openly offer corporate intelligence services. The most important is Intertel, a Florida-based organization employing former senior officials from virtually every intelligence and law-enforcement agency in the country. Intertel's agents include quite a few ex-CIA operators.

A former CIA official whom I know and who is intimately familiar with the workings of the system, remarked to me not long ago that this emerging industrial-intelligence complex is more pernicious than the military-industrial complex about which Eisenhower warned when he left the White House in 1961. This complex operates in a variety of ways. The oil companies, for example, have highly professional intelligence units that may rival government intelligence services. Their interest, of course, is in what their competitors are doing or planning—in searching for new sources of oil, making international arrangements, marketing decisions, and so on. The oil companies' international operations even penetrate the governments of petroleum-producing countries. On another level, the traditional practices of plain industrial espionage are being quietly replaced with long-range intell'gence schemes which may include planting agents in the employ of a competitor. It is no longer a question of stealing or illicitly buying the latest secret design, but of obtaining on a sustained basis top-secret corporate information concerning policies and decision-making processes. Agents are infiltrated into rival corporations and allowed to rise in the executive ranks to the point where all relevant information is available to them. This is the transfer to corporate life of the infiltration techniques of the CIA, MI-6, or KGB. It is always a major coup for an intelligence service to insert a "deep-cover" agent into the intelligence agency of another country.

The higher the agent rises in the organization in which he was planted, the more valuable he is to his real employers. The United States scored brilliantly in this field when Oleg Penkovsky, a KGB colonel, performed for years as an agent for the CIA and the British before being finally caught. The Russians had their triumphs with Otto Johns, the head of the West German intelligence service, who defected to Russia in the mid-1950s to avoid exposure. They also had a valuable investment in three British intelligence agents—Harold (Kim) Philby, Guy Burgess, and Donald McLean—who reported for years to the KGB before fleeing to Moscow when they were about to be discovered by Western counterespionage. Infiltration, then, is the latest corporate intelligence technique adapted from government operations. It poses the same ethical problems as general intelligence work, but the ex-CIA men now in the private sector seem to have no qualms about it all.

Howard Hunt fits in a special way into this category of intelligence operators who are never reconciled to the fact that they no longer belong to the CIA. As it happened, Hunt found himself doing classical intelligence work for the White House, as did McCord and the Cuban-Americans from Miami, who also had CIA ties in the past; but if this opportunity had not arisen, he might have easily gone into corporate intelligence work. At one point, in fact, he tried to link himself with the interests of the billionaire Howard Hughes, who maintains a security and intelligence operation of his own.

Finally, there are the ex-CIA technical experts who find work in private-detective or security firms or are hired by corporations in such endeavors as plant protection. These are the "nuts-

and-bolts" men who were never engaged in actual intelligence work. A case in point is James McCord, who set up a security firm in a Washington suburb after leaving the CIA in 1970. He also became security chief for the Republican National Committee and the Committee to Re-Elect the President—both of which were the principal clients of McCord's company.

A great many CIA employees simply retire and mind their own business. I have several friends who have done just that, and they have no hankerings after intelligence operations. When Hunt was recruiting personnel for his White House "horrors" team, as former Attorney General John N. Mitchell called the secret operation, several former CIA colleagues turned him down cold. But a California lawyer, also a CIA alumnus, actively helped him when he was in hiding, immediately after the Watergate break-in. And no matter what the CIA's officials testified to in the Senate Watergate hearings, there *is* such a thing as a CIA "old-boy network." It was quite helpful to Howard Hunt when he needed assistance.

Men like Hunt are curiously frozen in the past. Twenty-five years before Watergate, Hunt and many others made a commitment to certain ideas, ideologies, and a modus vivendi. In a sense, they also committed themselves to certain techniques, which once upon a time seemed to function perfectly in an imperfect world. The world went on changing, as it must, every day, week, month, and year, but the Hunts of our time did not follow the evolution. They were bypassed by history, and this lies at the root of their tragedies. This is perhaps why Hunt is now in a federal prison.

By 1973, most of the world has come to terms with the notion that communism is not a monolithic force and that it has many faces. President Nixon has gone to Peking and to Moscow. Leonid I. Brezhnev has come to Washington. The whole East-West relationship has undergone an astounding transformation. But there are men—men with the commitments that Howard Hunt made for the better part of his adult life—who resist change. To them, the CIA—and, to their way of thinking, the world—is tragically no longer what it used to be. Hunt himself has said this to friends and has made this point in his latest novel—published when he was already languishing in prison, the victim of a society he no longer could understand.

But the changes in the CIA started long before Watergate. Already by 1961, when President Kennedy came into office, new winds were blowing in the intelligence community. Even in the narrow context of its anticommunism, the vocational religion of the CIA, the notion was developing that in this increasingly sophisticated world communism must be opposed subtly and intelligently. Simple spying and "dirty tricks" were no longer good enough. Agents like Hunt might still have been involved in "black" operations, but in Washington new ideas were taking shape.

For example, in the closing years of the Eisenhower administration the Agency decided to move effectively in the field of culture. Covertly, as it does all things, the CIA undertook to finance the Congress for Cultural Freedom and a group of first-rate intellectual magazines such as *Encounter* in London, *Der Monat* in West Germany, *Preuves* in France, and others. The idea was to encourage non-Communist liberals and "progressive" groups, on the theory that it was disastrous for the United States to be wedded exclusively to right-wing groups or publications. This was, to be sure, an act of political manipulation, but as one of the senior Agency people engaged in this covert intellectual enterprise explained to me, the United States simply could not go on being identified with clearly reactionary forces such as the *patronat* organization of wealthy employers in France, at a time when the Communist party was building up strength in the labor unions. By the same token, it was felt that American views no longer should be exclusively reflected in newspapers around the world receiving secret CIA subsidies and identified with rightist causes. New generations have come to the fore, he said, and we had to adapt our approach to their intellectual and social requirements and caliber. So a new flexibility, annoying to the old-timers, came into being.

At home, the CIA, slightly overstepping its statutory role, managed to subsidize a highly active publishing house in New York without insisting that it stay away from liberal manuscripts or even criticisms of the Agency. This cultural effort was primarily engineered by two men—Robert Amory, then the CIA's Deputy Director, and Cord Meyer, a brilliant but unpredictable operator who in his earlier years was an active advocate of world federalism. In the ironic manner in which people respond to things, the CIA came under heavy criticism from American liberals in the mid-1960s for its underwriting of the Congress for Cultural Freedom, the intellectual magazines, and the New York publishing house. Yet it seems to me that this was in many ways a positive contribution from the Agency's treasury. Had the money come from the State Department, there would have been little outcry, even though the same taxpayer money goes into the coffers of both the CIA and the State Department. But at the other end of the spectrum, the Hunt generation in the CIA found it objectionable that the Agency was embarking on such peculiar schemes when, they felt, it could be concentrating on better and better "black" operations, taking advantage of the new technology that could be applied to clandestine crafts. Another former senior CIA official complained to me that the Agency was being destroyed because its new management was getting away from classical clandestine work in favor of the new technology, as manifested by orbiting satellites and a whole new arsenal of electronic intelligence. This particular man, who devoted most of his career to clandestine operations from Asia to the Soviet borders, was nevertheless prepared to accept the changing nature of intelligence without going to irrational extremes as some others had done.

But now, against this background, one must look at a man like Howard Hunt. He retired from the CIA in 1970, his final period of service consisting of irrelevant tasks given him so that he could serve out his time and qualify for a pension. Once out of the CIA, Hunt—and there are others—was like a fish out of water. He felt useless and frustrated, both as an individual and as an intelligence operative. This made him the natural candidate for the kind of domestic intelligence plan that the White House was beginning to put into effect. And when—a year after his retirement from the CIA, a year of unhappiness and emptiness—Hunt was recruited by the White House for its undercover operations, it was only natural that he should bring to this new assignment all the techniques of black propaganda and covert political action that he had employed for so many years against the foreign "enemies" of his country. The tragic difference, or the tragic misunderstanding, was that in his new capacity Hunt was turning these weapons and techniques against fellow Americans at home.

The way Hunt went about his new job could be called pathetic, had it not been part of a scheme of extraordinary danger to the welfare of the United States. He arranged secret interviews with the CIA's top men, this time arriving at the CIA Executive Office with a White House mandate. He behaved like the caricature of a secret agent. He procured from the CIA a silly wig, a tiny camera to be hidden in a tobacco pouch, false identification papers, and, of all implausible things, a speech-altering device. He wrote letters to fellow ex-CIA agents to lure them to join his fantasmagoric operations with offers of cash payments. He turned to his former Cuban-American associates from the days of the Bay of Pigs invasion and, counting on their special brand of loyalty, fitted them into a madcap operation that led to prison terms for two of these old comrades and for two others who were added to his improbable task force.

It is perhaps understandable, if one cares to understand such things, why Hunt acted in this fashion, never doing openly what could be done secretly, basking in the glory of the new intrigue, and reliving the good old days of conspiracy. But what cannot be so readily understood is that in Richard Nixon's Washington there was a demand for a man like Howard Hunt and for the kind of services that he would readily and gleefully perform. This, naturally, is the crux of the whole Watergate matter.

There was a President's staff, willing and prepared to procure for themselves a private intelligence service in order to satisfy their immediate political needs, as well as to help them cope with a society in ferment, whose acts of dissent seemed to petrify the American Presidency even more than the whole nuclear arsenal controlled by President Nixon's new partner in the world chess game, Secretary General Brezhnev.

With the whole intelligence community in a state of general disarray because of the way in which Nixon was running the government, a situation had arisen in which the formation of a private investigating unit in the White House made sense to its occupant. Key men in the Nixon administration embarked on a policy of undermining both the CIA and the FBI. A lot of it was just plain politics at its worst. But some of it was because the White House was being frustrated in its efforts to control the aging J. Edgar Hoover and to subordinate the CIA to the foreign-policy formulations emanating from the all-powerful National Security Council.

Under Nixon and his Special Assistant for National Security, Henry Kissinger, the White House set out to do away with the basic principle laid down in the creation of the CIA in 1947—its independence in presenting its judgments to the ultimate policy-maker of the nation. I like to believe that even such old war horses as the late Allen Dulles would not have taken kindly to the controls that Nixon and Kissinger tried to impose on the CIA.

The casual observer in the 1970s could not possibly have been aware of the political struggle which was undercutting both the foreign and the domestic intelligence agencies. Even with the limited perspective that one already has on these events, it seems almost beyond comprehension how the Nixon White House could have played political games with the intelligence community and the FBI, undermining both for reasons that could not possibly benefit national interests and national security, the very objectives that the President continuously invoked in almost every context of American political life.

But it became tragically logical that the men whom the President's staff got to conduct their private intelligence operations—behind the back and over the heads of the FBI and the CIA—should be frustrated intelligence adventurers such as Howard Hunt and his literal partner in crime G. Gordon Liddy, the one-time FBI agent with delusions of grandeur. At the age of fifty-three, Howard Hunt, hungry for prestige, power, and money, became in this manner the chief operative in an insane game of underhanded and undercover politics which the Presidency was then mounting. This thin, sandy-haired man, with the most easily forgettable of faces, became one of the co-architects of what might have been an American police state if he had not blown the whole operation out of the water through extraordinary careless-ness, arrogance, and overconfidence.

THE OBSESSION

1

The fatal flaw in the execution of the final Watergate raid, attributable to Howard Hunt, may well have been a consequence of the fact that he had never really worked as an espionage agent. In the nearly twenty-three years Hunt spent with the CIA, he was always a clandestine political operator, which is quite distinct from being an agent. It is a question of skills.

The CIA's Directorate of Plans—the clandestine services—has a wide variety of functions. All of the Directorate's work is covert, or secret, but modern clandestinity is divided into many categories and compartments. In the classical sense of espionage, sabotage, or special intelligence efforts, the CIA assigns specially trained personnel to specific tasks. Both at the headquarters buildings in Langley, Virginia, a few miles from downtown Washington, and in the "field" there are men and women known in CIA parlance as "case officers" who concentrate on undertakings that may range from pure spying to assassination (when needed); infiltration of foreign governments, intelligence services, and other organizations; larger enterprises such as the overthrow of governments; or paramilitary operations in cooperation with weapons and training specialists.

A case officer may often also be a "control officer," or "agent handler." This means that he maintains contact with American or foreign nationals who are not actually CIA employees but are in its pay, sometimes for many years. In an agent network, the handler may be the recipient of information flowing from informants and tipsters—this is quite a notch below agents on a permanent payroll, and these persons receive payment for specific duties accomplished.

Every American embassy overseas, and most consulates, include a CIA "station." This is a virtually independent CIA unit inserted in the embassy with the knowledge of the State Department and the local ambassador or chief of mission. The station functions publicly, in a relative sense. Its members are listed as diplomats, with all the privileges this entails. (From the CIA's inception, embassies have thus served as "covers."* In theory, the CIA station chief must keep the ambassador informed of all his activities, but he has his own classified line of communications—a backchannel—to CIA headquarters in Washington, bypassing the State Department. Quite frequently, CIA station chiefs have been known to ignore ambassadors altogether and to keep them in the dark about their operations. This is sometimes dictated by what CIA perceives to be overwhelming security reasons—it believes that even the ambassador has no real need to know what the Agency knows—and sometimes because of the personality of the CIA man at the foreign post.

The degree of strict controls maintained by the White House and the State Department over the CIA's clandestine army in Laos has long been a question of some debate. The Agency's critics claim that the vast CIA operation, supported by its private airline, Air America, was a freebooting operation. Others insist that every decision affecting the Meo army under General Vang Pao was subject to approval by American ambassadors in Vientiane—first William H. Sullivan and subsequently George McMurtrie Godley—who in turn reported fully to the Secretary of State and the President.

Obviously, the whole secret Laos operation was initially approved by President Johnson when it was first launched, and then reconfirmed by President Nixon. American officials who have served in Laos say that the clandestine army's operations as well as American air strikes in the south were the subject of a daily staff meeting, six days a week, involving the American ambassador, his deputy, the military and air attachés, and the CIA station chief. The Laotian general whose troops operated in the Plaine des Jarres often requested air support, ground supplies or American advisers, and the embassy team occasionally approved

---

* CIA men are listed in the State Department Biographic Register as reserve foreign service officers, which may help a discerning reader of embassy rosters to determine who may belong to a CIA station.

and occasionally rejected these requests.

It has also become known that during the early 1970s the CIA used the Agency for International Development (AID) as a cover for some of its operations connected with the clandestine army. Hospital and health care for wounded Meo soldiers came out of AID funds, and AID personnel were often involved in support operations for General Vang Pao's army. This presumes, of course, that the decision to involve AID in clandestine work was made at the highest levels in Washington.

As a rule, no effort is made to hide the true identities of CIA station chiefs in foreign nations and even some of his subordinates from the host governments. In friendly countries, this makes it easier for CIA station chiefs to cooperate with local intelligence and law-enforcement agencies. In the case of close American allies—the British, the Israelis, or the West Germans—there are clearly defined secret intelligence and liaison agreements. There is a flow of intelligence among members of the North Atlantic Treaty Organization under the "Interface" system, which, at least in theory, provides for interchange of intelligence among alliance members. Even senior American and Soviet intelligence officers have had occasions to meet and to chat informally about their work. This has become particularly true in the recent years of détente. Obviously, the CIA keeps a roster of every possible Soviet and other agent or top intelligence official it can identify, and the KGB and other services do likewise. Since intelligence is a sophisticated art, it has simply become more practical for each country to permit the presence in its midst of known foreign operatives—up to a tolerable point. This approach has the advantage of making it easier in some instances for the host government to keep track of semi-covert intelligence operators in the hope that such surveillance may lead to more interesting discoveries. Besides, since intelligence services are bound to go on existing anyway, there is a tacit gentlemen's accord among most of them to live and let live—so long as it does not get out of hand.

A classic example occurred in the 1960s, when the CIA assigned one of its top economic specialists to our Moscow Embassy and supplied the usual *curriculum vitae* on him, including the fact that he had served with the Agency. Though the American Ambassador in Moscow (it was then the late Llewellyn E. Thompson, Jr.) at first protested this departure from the "cover," out of his concern over Soviet reactions, he finally agreed. The Russians seemed to have enjoyed this episode immensely. As the story is told in the CIA, the economist (who held the rank of minister in the embassy) was openly and warmly received at the Soviet Economy and Agricultural Ministries, and Soviet officials often kidded him about whether he was carrying a hidden camera on him. And of course there are many American ambassadors with career CIA backgrounds. Most recently, Richard Helms left his post as CIA Director to become ambassador to Iran. And the new ambassador to Laos, Charles S. Whitehouse, is a former senior Agency official.

Parallel with CIA stations, there are "deep-cover" nets in a great many foreign countries. Often, they have no communications ever with the embassy station and operate entirely on their own under direct, clandestine instructions from Washington or one of the regional CIA commands. (Following the military pattern, CIA operations abroad are divided into commands, which are regionally controlled programs. Tokyo is the headquarters of the CIA's North Asia Command; the Indochina operation, naturally, is centered in Saigon. Paris was for many years the site of the European Command, but this was moved to London after France left NATO and the CIA became concerned over the security of its operations; Bonn was for a long time the Command for the Soviet Union and Eastern Europe. Mexico serves as the regional Command for Latin America.) These regional commands exercise a degree of supervision over both CIA stations in the embassies and some of the collateral covert operations. Not infrequently, there may be a deep-cover station chief in a foreign country in addition to his colleague in the American embassy. He is the man who runs agents' nets and engages in other black operations. A famous case of such a parallel structure came to light with the CIA's successful digging of a tunnel in Berlin in 1954 and 1955 in order to tap the underground center of Soviet military and intelligence communications. Only after the Russians accidentally discovered the tunnel fourteen months later did the CIA inform James B. Conant, then Ambassador to West Germany, that this enterprise was, indeed, an achievement of our intelligence.

The deep-cover CIA chief in a foreign country has his Soviet counterpart in the KGB's *rezident*. Colonel Rudolf Abel, discovered by American counterespionage in the late 1950s, was one of the most famous Soviet *rezidents*. One does not talk about who the American *rezidents* abroad might have been in the past or are today.

In any event, Howard Hunt never held such posts. With one exception—when he was CIA station chief in Uruguay—he was never engaged full time in the handling of actual intelligence work and certainly not in agentry. His specialty was so-called covert political action, and he worked out of various embassies under a State Department cover, unless he was at headquarters in Virginia. Hunt's mission was to specialize in covert political activities—*as distinct* from actual espionage or sabotage—and in black propaganda. This meant infiltrating political parties and organizations such as labor unions and youth groups, and helping, often with money, the pro-American and anti-Communist elements in them. It entailed the secret financing of different foreign publications. All in all, this was the kind of political groundwork the CIA laid in many instances for a *coup d'état* in a foreign country. Regimes are not overthrown by cloak-and-dagger American agents furtively working the streets, but by the Agency's political apparatus, which, with its immense resources, can sometimes influence political events in a country. This was vital work from the CIA's viewpoint, but it did not make Howard Hunt a spy or even a real deep-cover operator. The few occasions when Hunt was forced to use a cover name came when he was engaged in political preparations for the overthrow of the Guatemalan government in 1954 and, again, when he served as political adviser to the CIA-financed Cuban Revolutionary Council in whose name ostensibly the Bay of Pigs invasion was carried out in 1961.

Hunt, therefore, was not an experienced action officer, or agent, and the "horrors" of Watergate were something of a novelty to him when it came to the execution of the plans. But Hunt did have a certain amount of covert military experience because of his service with an OSS unit in the Burma-China theater during the war. But that was guerrilla warfare—in which one either succeeded, and lived to see the success, or failed and usually died. A friend of mine, with both OSS and CIA experience, remarked recently when we were discussing Hunt, "You know, it was much easier to be a guerrilla against the Japanese than to run the kind of bastard espionage-intelligence operation that Howard was attempting to do here. . . . Aside from physical danger and discomfort, believe me, it is easier to hide in the jungle than in Washington, particularly when you are linked to the White House and are reasonably well known in town."

It is not easy to reconstruct in detail the lives of covert CIA officers, and this is certainly true of Howard Hunt, who was given to elusiveness sometimes even beyond the call of professional duty. One knows a great deal about the famous leaders of the CIA—Allen Dulles, Dick Bissell, Tracy S. Barnes, Richard Helms, and so on—but the life stories of the Agency's anonymous operators are hard to piece together.

The State Department Biographic Register had until 1960 a brief entry summarizing Hunt's life from his birth in Hamburg, New York, on October 9, 1918, just a month before the end of World War I, to his ostensible retirement from the Foreign Service shortly before the Bay of Pigs. Hunt used this Foreign Service cover for most of his CIA career. There also is an entry on Hunt in *Who's Who in America,* which essentially repeats the information contained in the State Department directory and adds a few bits—such as the fact that he wrote forty-four novels (the forty-fifth came out in 1973) and once upon a time held a Guggenheim Fellowship in Mexico. But these dry official entries are contrived to cover rather than to illuminate the real story of Hunt's life. It is not, by the way, altogether unusual for CIA personnel to be listed in *Who's Who.* This is because the fat red books do list a large number of Foreign Service officers, even those below ambassadorial rank, when they appear to be interesting or important—or when a name is suggested by someone else who is already listed. Nonetheless, it is a curious touch of vanity that Hunt desired to be listed in *Who's Who*—one's cooperation is necessary—and this, too, tells us a bit more about the kind of man he is.

As a matter of policy, the CIA does not make available employment records of its employees, even the retired ones, because one might uncover in them a pattern of clandestine identities. Although I have many acquaintances, chiefly CIA and State Department officials, who at different times worked with or alongside Hunt, I found it rather astonishing how little they remembered about him—and, therefore, how little of an impression he must have made.

It may be unkind to say so at a time when Hunt is being

punished for criminal acts he had committed, but the record of my interviews with his former associates conveys the feeling that he was generally disliked and, in some instances, even held in something like contempt. Seeking recognition and approval, as we all do, he evidently sought in a variety of ways to compensate for the fact that he never really rose very high in the CIA and that he was far from being a favorite among his peers. This may well be the reason why Howard Hunt developed an intense and aggressive personality, although, when convenient, he could be ingratiating; why over the years he presented strange behavior patterns; and, in the end, why he slaved over his typewriter for years to produce so many books. Even though most of his novels (thus far he has written only one nonfiction book) were written under pen names, he must have hoped for some form of wealth and recognition from this toil in the subliterary vineyard.

It is likewise difficult to reconstruct Hunt's early life. He has no known living relatives except his children, and the kin on his wife's side, her first cousins, know virtually nothing of Hunt's youth. Since Hunt has very few close friends, there are limited sources for research into his youth. Being in prison, he refuses to be interviewed in depth. A man I know who worked with Hunt in the CIA in Latin America, vaguely remembers him from a summer camp around Buffalo, New York, where they both had gone in the 1920s, but he has no specific recollections. So the pattern repeats itself: the man whom nobody seems to remember. There are two or three men who, for a variety of reasons, have been close to Hunt over the years and might have been able to flesh out the bare skeleton of his biography. But they do not now wish to reminisce about Hunt. Others can contribute only bits of knowledge and strands of gossip.

What is known is that Howard Hunt was born in Hamburg, in upstate New York in 1918, the only child of Everette Howard

Hunt and Ethel Jean Totterdale Hunt. Hunt was named after his father, who was a lawyer and might have held a judgeship somewhere at some point in his life. Hunt's infancy was spent in the Buffalo area, but by 1926, when the Florida land boom was at its peak, Hunt Senior went to practice law in Miami Beach. Hunt briefly recollects this period in his book on the Bay of Pigs, to make the point that his association with Cuba dates back to his childhood.

But through this reference Howard Hunt also provides interesting insights into his attitude toward his father—obviously admiration—and into his general approach to life. His father had been practicing law in Florida, he writes,

with a partner who was given to drink, womanizing, and gambling. One Saturday morning, quite by chance, my father had occasion to visit his office and opened the firm's safe where he found $5,000 in cash missing.

A few inquiries told him that his partner had taken the night boat to Havana, so my father pocketed his Army Colt .45, chartered a seaplane and flew to Havana where he encountered the absconder in Sloppy Joe's bar. Father's intervention was direct, illegal and effective, for he flew back to Miami with most of the missing funds, and on Monday morning dissolved the partnership.

Although they went their separate ways, the two men remained friends throughout their lives. In the Cuban context the moral is, I suppose, that an operation conducted with surgical efficiency and maximum speed leaves minimal scars on those involved.

Howard Hunt was only eight years old at the time. But as he looked back on his work for the Bay of Pigs, he found it necessary to insert this vignette about his father, clearly to make the point that he believed in efficient operations, even if "illegal," and in "surgical" speed in solving problems. One perhaps understands better why Hunt rushed with such dedication into operations for the overthrow of foreign governments and even recommended to the CIA a plan to assassinate Cuba's Premier Fidel Castro. It all was "surgical."

At the age of eighteen, in 1936, Hunt entered Brown University after graduating from the Hamburg High School. Brown is an Ivy League college, but Hunt evidently had aspired to go to one of the more famous ones. In his book about the Bay of Pigs, he has a number of references to men he knew and admired who went to, say, Harvard; and in his novels, the hero (usually quite autobiographical) will have attended Yale, Princeton, or Harvard, the latter being the favorite. In one Hunt novel, the hero attends a famous prep school in Switzerland—and one wonders whether Hunt got this idea from the fact that Richard Helms was an alumnus of Le Rosey, the most famous of Swiss private schools.

Sometime in 1938, Hunt spent a short vacation in Havana. He wrote that this was "an escapade I remembered with affectionate nostalgia (despite the hepatitis it had brought)." He also spent a prewar summer in France. Hunt graduated from Brown with a B.A. degree in 1940. It is noteworthy that although he was an English major, he went in heavily for classics. He took Latin and Ancient Greek languages and literature, as well as several years of Spanish and courses in economics, psychology, and geology. His senior year was devoted entirely to English courses, as befitted a budding writer.

Perhaps the most important thing about being a Brown alumnus was that almost thirty years later it was to bring Hunt into association with another Brown man—a meeting that drastically changed Hunt's life. The fellow alumnus was Charles W. Colson, a Washington lawyer who was to become President Nixon's Special Council. Hunt and Colson were not at Brown at the same time. Colson is thirteen years younger than Hunt and graduated from the university thirteen years after Hunt completed his studies.

Late in 1940, Hunt seemed to be wondering what to do with his life. He was twenty-two years old and, aside from certain talents for writing and a love of excitement and adventure, had no set goals. Probably because of this sense of adventure—and because he evidently was not ready to embark on a career—Hunt joined the Navy, spending some eighteen months aboard ships. He was a sailor and, according to incomplete records, was injured aboard a ship doing Atlantic convoy duty and discharged from the Navy in 1942. The United States was already at war with the Axis powers.

It is unclear what precisely Hunt did during the following year. His official biography indicates that he was a movie script writer for unidentified producers, and editor of March of Time newsreel films, and, finally, a South Pacific war correspondent for *Life* magazine. If, indeed, he served as a war correspondent, it was for a very short period during 1943. Among my friends at Time, Inc., I could find no recollection of any man named Howard Hunt who was a war correspondent.

The year 1943 marked the start of Hunt's career in clandestinity. It was the turning point in his life, although friends were to say later that it was during the war years that Howard had first "flipped."

It is unclear, as so many other things are about Hunt's life, under what circumstances he joined the Office of Strategic Services. At that time, the OSS was already well established all over the world, drawing its personnel from both military and civilian sources. To the extent that this episode in his life can be reconstructed, Hunt volunteered for the Army Air Corps in 1943, and was assigned, first as a student and then as instructor, to the Air Force Intelligence School at Orlando, Florida. At some point in late 1943, he volunteered for the OSS and was quickly trained in clandestine intelligence work.

Hunt's time in the OSS is also unclear. Some information indicates that he was attached to an OSS unit in Southeast Asia which won a Presidential citation. Hunt may have belonged to this OSS Detachment No. 101, but it is by no means certain. The 101, which fought in Burma with local guerrillas and distinguished itself in defeating superior Japanese forces, is the only OSS Detachment to have received a Presidential citation. (It was at one time commanded by William R. Peer, who later became a Lieutenant General and was in charge of investigating the My Lai massacre in the Vietnam war.) I know quite a few of the 101 Detachment veterans, but none of them remembers the face or the name of Howard Hunt.

According to Hunt's former lawyer William O. Bittman, Hunt was in an OSS unit working with bands of Chinese guerrillas. This would have been OSS Detachment No. 202. Bittman once told me about Hunt volunteering to attack a Japanese unit in order to prevent the massacre of some American prisoners by their captors. In his book on the Cuban invasion, in which he occasionally reminisces about other situations in his past, Hunt mentions being at Kunming airport, in southeastern China. Kunming was the terminal for the airlift flights "over the Hump" from Burma which provided support for anti-Japanese forces in southern China. It was at Kunming that Hunt appears to have met for the first time Tracy Barnes, a remarkable OSS and later CIA officer, under whom Hunt was later to serve in the overthrow of the Guatemalan government and at the Bay of Pigs. Actually, Barnes, who died in 1972, spent most of the war in OSS detachments in Europe, but apparently he was on a temporary mission in Asia when he met Hunt.

It may be of some interest to note that among the officers of OSS Detachment 101 was Clark MacGregor, later a Congressman, a White House staffer, and, after the Watergate break-in, the replacement for John Mitchell as head of the Committee for the Re-Election of the President. Whether or not Hunt knew Mac-Gregor in some OSS capacity is not known. However, at the end of the Burmese campaign a number of OSS officers from Detachment 101 were shifted to Detachment 202 in China, and many of them parachuted into Japanese cities to supervise the surrender of Japanese garrisons. Yet the people from Detachment 101 have no recollection of Hunt in China, either. A leading member of the 101 said that it was essentially composed of seventy-five or so American officers who knew each other intimately and that it was inconceivable that Hunt would not have been known to the group had he been with them at some stage.

According to the official record, Hunt left the OSS as a First Lieutenant in the Army Air Corps in 1946. He obtained a Guggenheim Fellowship sometime during 1946 and spent close to a year in Mexico learning more Spanish and writing books. He had already written a few wartime spy thrillers, and evidently the Guggenheim committee considered him to be of some promise. This was Hunt's first exposure to Latin America, except for his student visit to Havana in the late 1930s.

Hunt's first and probably best book, *East of Farewell*, was published by Alfred A. Knopf in 1942. It was written when he was recovering from injuries suffered aboard the Navy ship, just before he joined the OSS. *East of Farewell* received very favorable reviews, and a New York publisher who then knew the author told me recently that this first book, written when Hunt was only twenty-four years old, demonstrated well the case of "a writer with great promise which was never fulfilled."

Hunt's second book was *Limit of Darkness*, apparently based on his short assignment as a war correspondent. A reviewer assessed it succinctly: it "was not *The Naked and the Dead*, but it is a creditable war novel of the 'I-seen-it' variety so popular during the war."

Returning from Mexico, Hunt spent all of 1947 and the early part of 1948 back in the United States employed as a screen writer, though we do not know where or by whom. This period produced three more books. One, *Maelstrom,* in 1948, was based on Hunt's Mexican experience and had a hero fleeing from the United States to Mexico to escape a Senate investigation. (This was curious prescience. After the Watergate break-in, Hunt himself was advised by the White House to flee the United States to avoid investigations which, in time, were to include Senate hearings.) *Maelstrom* did quite well and, according to the publisher in New York, sold some 150,000 copies in paperback, which was not bad in those days. Also in 1948 he wrote *Stranger in Town,* stories of the French Resistance. In 1949 came *Bimini Run,* an adventure story built around a former Marine and a drifting gambler named Hank Sturgis. Interestingly, Frank Sturgis was twenty-three years later one of the Watergate raiders under Hunt's command. This real Sturgis is a former Marine who has led a life of extraordinary adventures. I have no idea whether or how Hunt might have known Sturgis before 1949, but it is not a very common name. Perhaps it was a coincidence. *Bimini Run* did well in the paperback trade, likewise selling around 150,000 copies.

Hunt wrote under his own name until he joined the CIA. Afterward he turned to pseudonyms: John Baxter, Gordon Davis, Robert Dietrich, David St. John. The last one was a combination of the first names of his two sons. Then Watergate ironically gave him back the use of his real name on book covers. Two of them came out in 1973 as he sat in the federal prison at Danbury, Connecticut. His Watergate notoriety started a Howard Hunt literary mini-cult.

During his time in the United States around 1947, Hunt had befriended Julius Fleischmann, the heir to the Fleischmann yeast fortune. He visited Fleischmann during the summer at his New England place, but the relationship was never clear. I knew Fleischmann (who is now dead) many years later, but he never mentioned Hunt. I don't recall any occasion for it.

It appears that Hunt joined the CIA very late in 1947 or in the early part of 1948. Again, we do not know what precisely led him to join the infant intelligence organization. We do know, of course, that Hunt was attracted to adventure and excitement, and, as for so many OSS people, for him the CIA was a natural next step.

Howard Hunt, then a thirty-year-old bachelor, arrived in Paris sometime in 1948—we do not know the precise date—under his newly acquired cover as a State Department reserve officer. Ostensibly, he was attached to the Economic Corporation Administration (ECA), the Marshall Plan organization, to perform liaison with the American Embassy. Actually, he belonged to the year-old CIA station in the French capital. One of the men running the ECA office at that time was Richard Bissell. As an Assistant Administrator of the ECA program, he spent much of his time in Paris. Some intelligence community insiders believe that Bissell was already working for the CIA and using the economic post as a deep cover. If so, he had to work hard, because he was in considerable evidence in connection with the reconstruction program, and he formally joined the CIA only in 1952. In a recent conversation, Bissell, now an aircraft company executive, told me he had no recollection whatsoever of Hunt in Paris, although naturally he knew him during the Bay of Pigs episode in 1961.

ECA's principal political objective was to strengthen the European economies, in this instance the French economy, as part of the wider effort to block Communist expansion and penetration. The CIA was interested in precisely the same objective, and Hunt fitted well into the over-all operation. In this first of his CIA assignments, Hunt was chiefly involved in covert political activity and propaganda, with special emphasis on the French press and labor organizations. He had already acquired his rigorous anti-Communist attitude and made it perfectly clear to his embassy colleagues, as some of them remember to this day, where he stood politically and what he thought of State Department "liberals" who, in his judgment, were too soft on communism.

Even liberal priests bothered him. Himself a devout Roman Catholic, Hunt held the "worker priests" of Western Europe in deep contempt and later was to fear that their influence would spread to Latin America. As he wrote subsequently, "I recalled the 'worker priests' in France and Italy so many of whom were fellow travelers, and of the frankly subversive work in which they engaged."

But there was more than intelligence work in Paris in 1948, especially for an American bachelor with valuable dollars and access to the well-stocked embassy commissary. One of Hunt's close friends was Ionie Robinson, a painter and one of the most popular American women in Paris in those days. He certainly enjoyed the pleasures of Paris, and there seems to be no question that sex and alcohol—both of them in every conceivable dimension—were much on his mind. Friends who remember him from those days say that Hunt when sober was a rather introspective and quiet person, probably with a series of inferiority complexes. He would become agitated only on the subject of politics, particularly when he suspected that someone in the embassy or among Frenchmen was in some manner assisting what he saw as the Communist conspiracy. Then he would explode. When he drank, the same friends recall, he became much more forthcoming and humorous and, with women, even aggressive. Slim and thin-faced, Hunt somehow was not cut in the image of the conquering sexual hero—and he probably knew it.

But nobody can really tell more about Hunt in Paris than he did himself in a novel entitled *A Foreign Affair*, published in

1954 under the pen name of John Baxter. The novel, covering his time in Paris and a brief stay in Vienna, sticks closely to autobiographical facts, as most Hunt books do. And it displays a peculiar mixture of politics and sex. The blurb on the novel's paperback edition tells it all: "Here is more than a love story. Here is a searching behind-scenes look at Europe today—the tired but traditional culture of the continent in conflict with the dynamic and practical Americans who are determined to make it change. . . . He had wanted her from the first moment they had met, needed the soft warmth of her against him and the feel of her lips on his." And so on.

The hero, Michael Prentice, happens to be an American diplomat attached to the ECA. He is a hard-drinking, handsome, and decidedly anti-Communist bachelor, battling his pro-leftist colleagues and carrying on a torrid love affair with a French countess, whose Spanish husband was believed to have died in Russia as an officer with the Blue Division that fought alongside the Nazis in World War II. (Hunt's acquaintances say that his real romantic life was not quite so flamboyant and his interest in sex was highly intellectual or sublimated. Many years later, according to his Cuban friends, Hunt spent a whole night in a Miami motel with a pliant young lady supplied by his hosts. But, she complained later, "All he did was to keep me up all night talking about his novels.") Michael is a suave connoisseur of fine food and wines. I cannot say how suave the real Hunt was in those days, but there is no question that, indeed, he knew his French foods and French wines as few foreigners do. Throughout the book the hero is continuously pouring himself shots of cognac, dropping a few francs on the *bistro* counter to pay for a drink, or sitting alone or with friends around a bottle of Scotch. When it comes to sex, the book borders on the pornographic. The author seems to have a strong interest in homosexual men and Lesbians, and the novel is full of incidents in homosexual bars and other situations involving male and female homosexuality. It should also be added that Hunt has a good ear for certain kinds of speech: his heroes sound exactly like Howard Hunt quoting himself in his book on the Bay of Pigs, written many years later.

On September 7, 1949, a little over a year after his arrival in Paris, Hunt married (over his parents' objections) a dark-haired young lady named Dorothy L. Wetzel, a secretary for the CIA station in Paris, also working under a State Department cover. Dorothy was born in Dayton, Ohio, but from the age of three she lived with her uncle and aunt because her parents were divorced and her mother evidently could not afford to take care of a young child. A quiet girl, with an intellectual bent, Dorothy went to a Cleveland high school and attended Bowling Green State University in Bowling Green, Ohio. Foreign languages were one of her greatest interests. She was an avid reader and she spoke French and Spanish fluently by the time she joined the CIA. Her interest in foreign lands and languages was probably what attracted her to the Agency.

One can readily imagine this reserved young girl becoming captivated by the dashing Howard Hunt. For his part, he probably made the most of his intellectual capacities to impress her. Excellently educated, Hunt had high literary aspirations. Almost incongruously, his espionage-cum-sex novels begin with epigraphs from such greats as Ezra Pound or Pliny the Elder. But we must remember that Hunt was a classicist.

In the winter of 1949–50 Hunt was sent on a temporary assignment to Vienna, leaving Dorothy behind in Paris. *A Foreign Affair* also describes his days in Vienna, still under four-power occupation. Michael Prentice continues as a bachelor but leaves his beloved lady behind in France, just as Howard had Dorothy waiting for him in Paris. For Michael, Vienna is again the scene of complicated sexual liaisons, hard drinking, and political work. Hunt carefully refrains from any mention of the CIA or intelligence work in general in this book, by the way. The hero's friends are American colonels and senior diplomats, and, of course, he has run-ins with the Soviets.

In real life, Vienna was a crucial point for CIA operations, not only from the viewpoint of consolidating Western positions in Austria, but also because the CIA used that city as a principal observation and action base for Eastern Europe and the Soviet Union. In those days Vienna was one of the places where intelligence wars were fought at their most intensive. Hunt stayed with his specialty of covert political action, concentrating once more on newspapers, public opinion, and civilian organizations. The name of the game, naturally, was to influence the Austrians in favor of the West and against the Soviet Union—this was before the peace treaty was concluded and Austria proclaimed a neutral state. Hunt rubbed elbows with all kinds of CIA and military intelligence agents and Vienna was one of the crucibles in which his personality was molded.

Sometime in 1950, Hunt was ordered back to CIA headquarters, then located in temporary buildings—known as "Quarters Eye"— not far from the Lincoln Memorial in Washington. Dorothy returned with him to the United States, and their first child, Lisa, was born in 1950.

Hunt's Latin American career began later in the same year when the CIA assigned him to the station in the American Embassy in Mexico City. Both he and Dorothy spoke Spanish, and it seemed like a good posting for Hunt, as he slowly made his way up the ladder of the clandestine division. The Hunts arrived in Mexico City on December 13, 1950, and Howard joined the large CIA station there under the orders of the late Winfield Scott. Mexico City, the CIA's regional command in Latin America, was a fairly busy place for CIA agents not only because of the always volatile political situation in Mexico, but also in terms of the shifting politics of Central America and the Caribbean. But Hunt, whose specialty continued to be covert political action, found time to work on his novels, and *A Foreign Affair* was written there. Also in Mexico, the Hunt's second child, a daughter named Kevan, was born in 1952.

For nineteen months in 1951 and 1952, Hunt had under his orders William F. Buckley, Jr., who later became the well-known syndicated conservative columnist. Buckley was in Mexico for the CIA on what he recently described as a "tangential special project." They quickly befriended each other, and Buckley is the godfather of three Hunt children. He remains to this day Hunt's best friend and was named the executor of Dorothy Hunt's estate after she was killed in a plane crash in 1972.

We don't know how effective Hunt might have been in Paris or Vienna, but in Mexico he became a bit of a fumbler, a trait that kept surfacing throughout his career. One typical incident happened sometime in 1953, when Ramón Magsaysay, the late President of the Philippines, arrived in Mexico on a world tour. Magsaysay's government was nearing victory over Huk guerrilla insurgents at home, and his unofficial escort on the trip was Colonel Edward G. Lansdale (now a retired general), who was probably the first serious American counterinsurgency expert and played a major role in Vietnam in subsequent years.

Because one of Hunt's responsibilities in Mexico were labor unions, he somehow contrived—and Howard was a master at contriving situations—to arrange for a meeting between Magsaysay and a Mexican labor leader whom the CIA was courting. The American government was then very concerned about the activities of Lombardo Toledano, a left-wing labor leader with a considerable following in Mexico and much of Latin America. The CIA and Hunt were naturally trying to develop non-Communist labor leadership in Mexico. The embassy was trying to do likewise through its regular labor attaché, and sometimes friction would develop between the embassy and Hunt about who was doing what. In any event, Lansdale was persuaded to have Magsaysay privately meet Hunt's labor leader, presumably to instill anti-Communist sentiments in him. It should be noted, however, that Magsaysay was riding a wave of popularity in the Philippines because of his new land reform and was considered to be quite progressive by Asian standards. A time was set for the meeting at a CIA "safe house" in Mexico, but Lansdale had the good sense to arrive an hour or so ahead of time to check out the house and take a good look at the Mexican labor leader. A few minutes later, the Mexican secret police raided the "safe house" to arrest the leader on charges ranging from pro-Communist conspiracies to criminal activities. Furious, Lansdale telephoned Hunt at the embassy and chewed him out for creating a situation which could have been of enormous embarrassment to the Filipino President.

Toward the end of his stay in Mexico, Hunt was pulled into the CIA's preparations for the overthrow of the Guatemalan President, Jacobo Arbenz Guzman, a left-wing figure whose policies and inclinations troubled Washington.

Late in 1953, a special CIA team for Guatemala was organized in Washington under Tracy Barnes—Harvard Law School graduate, OSS hero, and then a key man in the Agency's clandestine division. Barnes selected Hunt as chief of political action for the operation. Hunt's responsibility was to maintain contact with exiled anti-Arbenz leaders. Three of them, Colonel Carlos Castillo Armas, Colonel Miguel Ydígoras Fuentes, and Doctor Juan Córdova Cerna, were spending most of their time in neighboring Honduras. Hunt, working out of the Mexican station, kept in touch with them in Tegucigalpa, though he also held secret meetings at the Mexico City YMCA with Doctor Córdova, who was his candidate for provisional President when the Arbenz regime was overthrown.

From the outset, the CIA plan was to support and equip a band of rebels whom Colonel Castillo Armas had concentrated in Honduras. That little country and El Salvador were increasingly concerned with Arbenz's politics, and they made it clear to

Washington that they feared the spread of Guatemalan influence in their countries. But the single fact that determined U. S. action against Arbenz was the information, transmitted by CIA agents in East Germany, that a Swedish freighter, the *Alfhem,* was sailing for Guatemala with 15,000 crates of what was believed to be Czechoslovak arms for Arbenz. As the *Alfhem* sailed from the East German port of Stettin toward the Caribbean, CIA stations along the route kept Agency headquarters in Washington informed about her circuitous movements. All the messages went directly to Allen Dulles, then CIA Director. The Swedish freighter reached the Guatemalan port of Puerto Barrios on May 13, 1954. The following day, the CIA station in Guatemala City advised headquarters that the crates being unloaded from the *Alfhem* contained around 2,000 tons of small arms and ammunition as well as light artillery pieces. The immediate conclusion at the CIA was that Arbenz, now disposing of a considerable arsenal of arms, could dominate all of Central America and even endanger Panama and the Canal. The interpretation at the CIA was that with the arrival of the arms, the Soviet Union had secured a toe-hold in the Western Hemisphere.

On May 14, Allen Dulles summoned an emergency meeting of the Intelligence Advisory Committee, composed of himself as Director of Central Intelligence, the heads of the Army, Navy, and Air Force Intelligence, intelligence representatives of the Joint Chiefs of Staff, the Atomic Energy Commission, and the State Department. The Committee concluded that Arbenz was virtually certain to start an aggressive war in Central America. It was never made clear on what basis this conclusion was reached, but the intelligence community felt that the arrival of the Czechoslovak arms in Guatemala gave it the long-awaited excuse to move against Arbenz. On May 15, the National Security Council met at the White House, and Allen Dulles urged U. S. assistance to the rebels in Honduras. The National Security

Council decided to act. The American Ambassador in Guatemala City, the late John E. Peurifoy, took command of political operations. CIA paramilitary advisers as well as political operatives led by Howard Hunt set up operations in Tegucigalpa and in the Honduran jungles near the Guatemalan border where Colonel Castillo Armas had his rebel detachment. As Hunt wrote later, it was the arrival of the Swedish freighter in Guatemala that made the CIA set a date for the anti-Arbenz operation. On May 17, Secretary of State Dulles announced publicly that the United States had hard information that Communist arms had been delivered to Guatemala. This shipment was viewed by Washington with great concern, he said, because of its size and because it had come from a Communist country.

The following week, the Pentagon dispatched to Honduras and Nicaragua—this time without public announcements—two Air Force Globemasters with over twenty-five tons of rifles, machineguns, small arms, and ammunition. These arms were destined for Colonel Castillo's little army. The United States also quietly made available to the Colonel three old B-26 bombers. On June 16, the CIA's protégés launched the attack on Guatemala. The B-26s bombed and strafed Guatemala City, and Colonel Castillo's rebel band moved across the border into Guatemala. It was what Hunt would call a clean, surgical operation. Within five days, Arbenz was overthrown and fled the country. Many years later, he found refuge in Fidel Castro's Cuba.

The new Guatemalan President was now Colonel Castillo Armas. Hunt's candidate, Dr. Córdova, was no longer in the running because of a cancer operation he had undergone in Mexico. Hunt's own view was that in Córdova's absence the Presidency shsould have gone to Colonel Ydígoras Fuentes, whom he thought to be a better man, but according to Hunt the CIA paramilitary people from the clandestine division preferred Colonel Castillo. A few years later, Colonel Castillo was assassinated, and Ydígoras took over as President. He was to show his gratitude to the United States in 1960 when he made Guatemalan territory available for the training of the Cuban exiles who embarked on the Bay of Pigs invasion.

The CIA made no particular secret of its involvement in Guatemala. Faithful to its policy, it made no formal statements on the subject, but it never contradicted the widely circulating reports that it had played a central role in Arbenz's ouster. In fact, the Agency was quite proud of this operation, as Allen Dulles was to point out in his book nine years later.

Andrew Tully, a rather sympathetic observer of the Agency, wrote in his book *CIA—the Inside Story,* that "the Guatemala story shows CIA at its very best—in the gathering of information worldwide, in the communication of that information to headquarters and in its speedy evaluation for the guidance of policymakers. In other cases there is little doubt that CIA has violated its mandate by trespassing on policy-making, but in the Guatemala case—except for necessary inferences—it merely told its story to the National Security Council and from there the Defense Department took over." This, of course, is not accurate. As Hunt himself has written, the CIA had been preparing the Guatemalan operation long before the Swedish freighter sailed from Stettin for Puerto Barrios. Reflecting the official view, Tully wrote further,

The United States properly abhorred the idea of a Communist regime in the Western Hemisphere and felt it should do something to help Guatemalans to rid themselves of it. When the Communists shipped arms to Arbenz and thus involved international Communist conspiracy in the internal affairs of a Latin American country, it was the CIA which furnished the United States policy-makers with the vital intelligence that provided a most valid excuse for intervention. In this case, Allen Dulles did not have to press policy on the policy-makers; his intelligence was so accurately disturbing that there was only one thing the country could do.

Guatemala may have been successful from this viewpoint, but it also served to intoxicate the CIA with an overwhelming sense of power. Because Guatemala worked in 1954, it was decided six years later that a similar, though larger, operation would likewise triumph in Cuba. Thus, the fiasco of the Bay of Pigs was born from the victory in Guatemala.

Howard Hunt, his Guatemalan mission accomplished, returned to Washington to wait for a new assignment. That same year the Hunt's third child, St. John, was born. For Hunt, the Guatemalan operation had been a personal as well as a professional achievement. For the first time, he had tasted power, real power, and a sense of personal participation in destroying the demons of communism that he saw encroaching upon the Americas. This experience taught him conclusively that any operation conducted under the "proper authority" was valid even if it meant infringing on the sovereignty of a foreign country or, as it was to occur later, on the civil rights and privacy of individuals at home.

Guatemala also fitted into the larger pattern of intelligence combat developing all over the world. In Europe and Asia, the CIA was running extensive operations centered on the Soviet Union and China to penetrate their defense secrets (just as the KGB was trying to penetrate our defense secrets) and to weaken them politically in the areas immediately adjoining them. Agents were moved around or recruited to obtain maximal information about Soviet nuclear advances—the Soviet Union had exploded her first atomic bomb five years earlier—and deployed around the fringes of China. In Asia, the CIA effort was centered on strengthening the Nationalist Chinese on Taiwan, keeping an eye on Southeast Asia, turbulent as ever, and preventing the spread of Chinese communism in the region. The fact that the Chinese Communists crossed the Yalu River during the Korean War in 1950 convinced the United States that Peking had aggressive designs all over Asia, and the Agency was geared to counteract it.

One of the most important CIA operations in the China theater, based in Taiwan, had as a cover the innocent-sounding name of Western Enterprises, allegedly a commercial company in Taipeh. In Europe, similar dummy companies helped to maintain CIA covers.

At home, too, it was a time of intense anticommunism. It was the day of Senator Joseph R. McCarthy and his public offensive against all those in public or private life whom he suspected of the slightest inclination toward communism. Howard Hunt was in Washington during a part of the McCarthy period and, according to people who knew him well at the time, he admired and applauded the junior Senator from Wisconsin for his defense of "our institutions." At dinners in Washington, Hunt would carry on loudly in defense of McCarthy's tactics. As one of his friends was to say later, "Howard was a regular right-wing nut."

Even during the Guatemalan operation, Hunt had already acquired a new cover: as adviser to the Department of Defense in the capacity of a "POLAD" (Political Adviser) to the Department of the Army. Late in 1954, he was dispatched to Japan to join the Tokyo station in a covert political capacity. His official listing in the State Department's Biographic Register was that of a political officer attached to the Far East Command. It is customary for the State Department to attach legitimate political advisers to major military commands, and this was a perfectly credible cover for Hunt.

Tokyo was at the time the headquarters of the CIA's North Asia Command, which was responsible for Japan, Korea, and China. The operation included a clandestine staff for intelligence, and Hunt was assigned to the covert activities section of political action and propaganda. He served as deputy chief of a five-man staff specializing in black propaganda centered on Asia. The Korean War had ended the previous year, and the CIA, along with the rest of the United States government, felt that it was urgent to consolidate American political influence in Asia. Hunt's contribution was the manufacturing of propaganda directed against Communists; often this was what is known in the intelligence community as "disinformation," to be planted wherever it could be the most effective. As an author of thrillers, Hunt possessed the imagination required for this political task and, to the extent that anybody knows, he acquitted himself well.

Although Hunt was officially assigned to the Asian operation beginning late in 1954, he spent about a year in Washington serving on a secret CIA committee on psychological warfare in the Directorate of Plans. When the Agency needed someone for a particular assignment, it made no difference where the person might be: he was instantly summoned back to "Quarters Eye." The special committee was concerned with psychological warfare world-wide and Hunt was put in charge of Southeastern Europe: Albania, Yugoslavia, Bulgaria, Greece, and Turkey. Some of the hottest black CIA operations were then in progress in that region, and Hunt was instructed to deal with covert propaganda and political action. He had never before visited the area, but he immediately plunged into homework and flitted back and forth between Washington and the countries of Europe's "soft underbelly."

His former colleagues on the CIA committee remember Hunt as a dapper "wild man" with tremendous energy and imagination. He was self-confident, and, as one of his associates said later, "very much in his element in this black work." The CIA's political and psychological warfare operations at the time were divided into "gray" ones, which could be plausibly denied if the Agency were caught in mischief, and "black," which was outright deception. Hunt kept coming up with proposals that his superiors considered at best implausible. His imagination was overheated. One of his colleagues said subsequently that "Howard's thoughts were pure fantasy. . . . He thought black all the time." But the mid-1950s were the "era of *machismo*," as someone put it later, and one's standing in the CIA was measured by "how much you went after the gizzard of Communism. . . . What was wanted was zest."

During this Washington assignment Hunt shared an office in the CIA's clandestine division with Robert Cushman, then a Marine Corps colonel on temporary duty with the Agency. This acquaintance with the square-jawed Marine officer was to serve Hunt many years later in various situations, all the way up to Watergate.

During the mid-1950s Hunt was in Europe on several missions— some of them to do with Southeastern Europe, others possibly related to the new U-2 spy-plane program, then being launched under Richard Bissell's supervision. Hunt wrote later that he had a slight involvement with the U-2 project and was called upon on at least one occasion to arrange for landing and take-off rights for the CIA spy planes that crossed the Soviet Union from south to north and back again at altitudes over 60,000 feet to photograph Soviet military installations. In Europe, Norway was the terminal point for U-2 flights from Turkey or Pakistan, and the planes took off again from Norway for the return flight south. There are reasons to believe that Hunt was briefly charged with arranging U-2 facilities in Turkey.

Hunt returned to the United States in the latter part of 1956 and was once more attached to the CIA's Western Hemisphere division in clandestine services. In November, he went to Havana to attend the annual regional conference of CIA station chiefs in Central America and the Caribbean. A few officers, like Hunt, came from Washington headquarters. The meeting was presided by the American Ambassador to Cuba, Arthur Gardner. As Hunt later related the story, the CIA men, led by Colonel J. C. King, chief of the Western Hemisphere division, were saying their farewells to the Ambassador when an embassy official rushed up to tell Gardner that Cuba's President Fulgencio Batista had sent word that a small group of rebels had landed in Oriente Province, in eastern Cuba. The date was December 2, 1956, and the landing was under the command of Fidel Castro. Hunt recalls that when Castro's name was mentioned, Colonel King told the group that the Cuban rebel had been "heavily involved" in the 1948 riots in Bogotá, Colombia, during a conference of American foreign ministers. But, according to Hunt, there was no further discussion of Castro or his landing. It was obviously not being taken seriously.

Hunt was presently on his way to a new assignment as CIA station chief in Montevideo, Uruguay. This was the first and only time that Hunt served as a station chief. He arrived with his family in Montevideo on January 25, 1957, and proceeded to organize a pleasant life that combined political intelligence work with novel-writing. Montevideo was not the busiest CIA station in the world, although Hunt had to keep an eye on the activities of the large Soviet legation in the Uruguayan capital, which was then regarded as the center of Soviet and Communist propaganda and influence in South America. (The Soviet Embassy in Mexico presumably had the same task for that country and Central America.) There also were Uruguayan politics, but this could hardly take up much of Hunt's time. He and his family moved into a spacious house in the elegant Montevideo suburb of Carrasco, on the beach, near the city's most famous casino. Hunt had at his disposal a CIA-owned Cadillac, presumably for official business, and an MG sports car, which he owned. His cover at the embassy was that of a Political Section officer, though three months after his arrival he was promoted to the rank of first secretary in the Foreign Service reserve. His State Department colleagues from this period remember that Hunt spent a good deal of his time on the Montevideo cocktail circuit and producing more and more books.

In his book about the Bay of Pigs that he was to write in 1967, Hunt said that during his three years in Uruguay he had no special concern with Cuba. However, "I became accustomed to seeing groups of Cuban students and their partisans collecting funds in South America for Castro's 26th of July Movement, and because I was aware of Castro's communist background the sight made me uneasy. Even so, there were no orders from Headquarters to penetrate the pro-Castro groups abroad. Not even when on New Year's Day, 1959, Fidel took over the reins of government and established mass executions as the basic principle of revolutionary law." Before too long, however, Hunt became very deeply involved in Cuban affairs.

In the meantime, he engaged in a grotesque intrigue designed to protect his personal interests. Early in 1960, the CIA informed Hunt that he was being transferred back to Washington inasmuch as his three-year tour of duty in Uruguay was up. But this did not suit Hunt, who was enjoying the pleasant life in Carrasco and busily turning out his thrillers and sex novels. In the late winter of 1960, word came that President Eisenhower was planning a good-will trip to South America and that he would visit Uruguay in addition to Brazil, Argentina, and Chile. This was a little more than a year after Castro took power in Cuba, and the Eisenhower administration was eager to maintain and encourage pro-American sentiment in South America. Even then the United States was concerned that the Castro influence might spread southward.

With knowledge of Eisenhower's imminent trip, Hunt arranged to call on Uruguay's new President, Benito Nardone. He proceeded to explain to him that it would be damaging to the good relations between Uruguay and the United States if he, Hunt, were transferred. To say the least, it is unusual for a CIA official to turn to the president of a country where he is stationed to seek help in his own professional affairs. But Hunt, never troubled by ceremony, did just that. Specifically, he asked President Nardone to take up the question of his transfer to Washington during the Uruguayan leader's forthcoming meeting with Eisenhower. State Department officials say that Hunt then told Nardone's top advisers that he would arrange for the Uruguayan President to receive one or more of the helicopters that Eisenhower would be using on his South American tour. (The practice in Presidential travels was for a group of Marine Corps helicopters to be on hand ahead of time to transport the President from one point to another wherever he was visiting.) It is not known whether Hunt was actually hinting at bribing the Uruguayan government in this manner.

When Eisenhower arrived in Montevideo in the first days of March, Nardone conveyed Hunt's message to a totally astonished Eisenhower. Accustomed as he was to traditional military and White House staff systems, Eisenhower was taken aback by the notion that a relatively low-level CIA agent had engaged the President of a friendly country to speak on his behalf. That same evening, Eisenhower mentioned the incident to the American Ambassador, Robert F. Woodward. He did so with a sense of incredulity, but, at the same time, he made it clear to Woodward that he did not propose to get involved in CIA's staffing problems and that he would ignore the Uruguayan President's request. Shortly thereafter, word came from Washington for Hunt to return home as ordered. A new CIA station chief was about to arrive in Montevideo.

Hunt has his own version of the events that led to his departure from Montevideo. As he tells it in his book, "In March 1960 I was having coffee with the newly elected president of the country to which I was assigned, when a [CIA] station officer was admitted. He told me that an urgent cable was waiting for me at the American embassy, so I left and returned to my office. The cable said I was wanted at Headquarters the following day to discuss a priority assignment, and it was signed jointly by Richard Bissell, Chief of CIA's Clandestine Services, and his first assistant, Tracy Barnes."

One thing that Hunt omitted to relate in his account was that at the same time he was apparently seeking Nardone's help, he was secretly organizing a plot to overthrow the Uruguayan government. State Department officials say that Hunt considered Nardone to be somewhat too far to the left (actually he was what we would call a populist) and took it upon himself to start organizing a coup. This appeared to be Hunt's personal notion, inasmuch as neither the White House nor the State Department ever entertained such ideas, and there is nothing to indicate that even the CIA had an interest in it. In any event, Hunt set this conspiracy in motion behind Ambassador Woodward's back.

The job that was awaiting Howard Hunt in Washington in the spring of 1960 was part of a top-secret project, just approved by Eisenhower, to help Cuban exiles overthrow Fidel Castro by means of an armed invasion of Cuba.

To Hunt—fervent anti-Communist and convinced believer that Castro represented the most evil forces in the world—this was an ideal assignment, and he greeted it with joy. According to his own account, Hunt was told by Tracy Barnes that he was being designated "Chief of Political Action" in the invasion, and that his responsibility would be to forge Cuban exile leaders in the United States "into a broadly representative government-in-exile that would, once Castro was out, form a provisional government in Cuba." This was exactly the same sort of mission that Hunt had held in the Guatemalan effort six years earlier.

But concepts had changed since Guatemala, and even the CIA was aware of it. According to Hunt's own story, the CIA officer directly in charge of the operation told Hunt that "The only question raised about you is whether you're too conservative to handle guys like these. A lot of them are way to the left of you, socialists, labor leaders, and so forth." Hunt quoted himself as replying that, "I'm a career officer. I take orders and carry them out. My own political views, whatever they may be, don't enter into it." But this was not to be the case.

Aside from Barnes, Howard Hunt's immediate superiors in the project were Colonel King, chief of the Western Hemisphere division; the Project chief, known as "Jake"; and a German-born CIA official whose real name was Drecher but who went under the cover name of "Frank Bender." Bender was in charge of Political Action in general, and Hunt's special responsibility were exiled Cuban leaders whom the CIA was organizing as the Democratic Revolutionary Front.

Hunt spent a year on the project before he quit the operation in disgust over the "leftist" turn it was taking, and he watched the failure of the Bay of Pigs invasion from the sidelines in Washington. Despite assurances to his CIA superiors that his politics would not get in the way of his work, Hunt was so strongly motivated by rightist ideology that, in his own words, he was baffled that the exiled Cuban leadership would first be established clandestinely in Mexico. "Having served several years in Mexico I felt the leftist political climate was far from auspicious for our understanding. Besides, Castro and his 26th of July people were revered by most Mexicans and could count on the invaluable aid of . . . Marxist notables."

Even that early in the game, Hunt had bones to pick with a number of people in the United States government. He made a point of accusing Woodward (who as Ambassador in Uruguay had refused to help him with his efforts to remain in Montevideo) of having tried to "undercut" the CIA's effort in Guatemala, and in his book on Cuba, Hunt contemptuously quotes Woodward as telling him, " 'I hope you're not going to get into any of this Cuban business. It would be tragic if we went in there the way we did in Guatemala,' " Hunt was also unhappy that James Noel, who had been CIA station chief in Havana since before the Castro take-over, had been attached to the invasion project. The Havana station had helped a number of key anti-Castro leaders, such as Manuel Artime, to escape from Cuba, and he felt that "there was a certain ironic justice" in this, since Noel "and his deputy had been enthusiastic over Castro while he was in the Sierra Maestra, and had treated with certain rebel groups to the rage of Ambassador Earl E. T. Smith." Hunt also suggested that several liberally inclined State Department officials in charge of Latin American affairs "exercised considerable influence" over Colonel King. Even Bender, chief of the Cuban political operation, was on Hunt's list of undesirables. He was upset when Bender told him that both Bissell and Barnes disliked the old Cuban conservative element (although, according to Hunt, Vice President Nixon sympathized with them) and that post-Castro Cuba "would be entirely unlike the Cuba of Fulgencio Batista."

Thus, Hunt was caught in a curious trap. He was too right wing, even for the top people in the CIA, yet he had been handed the improbable task of organizing a Cuban political force that would be more liberal and progressive than the Batista dictatorship. Improbable as it was, Hunt's year-long involvement in the invasion project acquainted him with enough far-right Cubans in Florida so that more than ten years later he could turn back to these friendships.

In April 1960, Hunt changed covers. He went through the motions of resigning from the Foreign Service—his cover until then—and told friends and acquaintances that he had left the State Department to go and live in Mexico on a recent inheritance and to work on books. His first political assignment, however, was a secret trip to Madrid, where he undertook to convince the Cuban Military Attaché, Colonel Ramón Barquín, to defect from Castro's service. Barquín was a valuable officer, and it was thought at CIA headquarters that he would fit well into the invasion plans. He had been imprisoned by Batista for an earlier plot. But in those days, men like Barquín still remained faithful to Castro and the Colonel turned Hunt down flat.

The next idea was for Hunt to visit Havana to get a sense of the political situation there. CIA specialists provided Hunt with fake documentation supporting his cover. He flew from Tampa to Havana, and inevitably his first political conversation was with a taxi driver who, according to Hunt's memoirs, told him, " 'We can't go on like this. . . . No tourists now, and I can't get replacement parts for my taxi. There's a gas shortage. . . . I'll keep driving until the car gives out, then walk away from it.' " The driver told Hunt that he might in the end flee to Miami. This apparently convinced Hunt from the outset that Cubans were against Castro. And this, as it developed, was the broader judgment in the Agency back in Washington.

The next piece of Hunt's political research was at lunch at the American Club in Havana with the friend of another CIA agent, the owner of a small textile plant. He, too, was complaining. Hunt struck up conversations with such people as charter-boat captains and deck hands on the Havana docks, not to mention a former television dancer and entertainer whom he met through CIA contacts, and he found very few who favored the Revolution. Hunt also witnessed pro-Castro demonstrations in Havana streets. He concluded: "If I had doubts about the wisdom of our Cuban project, they were resolved . . . and I determined to dedicate myself to ridding Cuba of Castro and his henchmen, regardless of personal cost and effort." Cuba had become Hunt's personal crusade.

Back in Washington a few days later, Hunt submitted a series of recommendations to the CIA, beginning with the proposal to assassinate Castro before or coincident with the invasion. He called it "a task for Cuban patriots." The other recommendations called for the destruction of the Cuban radio and television transmitters before or during the invasion; the destruction of the island's microwave relay system just before the invasion; and a decision to avoid provoking a popular uprising against Castro until, as he put it, "the issue has already been militarily decided." Hunt, of course, was right that no uprisings should be started before the success of the planned invasion was assured, but it remains part of the intelligence mystery in the CIA why anyone thought that the invasion could succeed in the first place, and that an uprising at any point was possible.

Another mystery was why the CIA high command went on taking Hunt seriously. Quite clearly, there was no intention of assassinating Castro (as I noted earlier, such a plan needed the personal authorization of the President of the United States, and Eisenhower was reluctant to order political murder) and Hunt recorded plaintively, "As the months wore on I was to ask Barnes repeatedly about action on my principal recommendation, only to be told that it was 'in the hands of a special group.' So far as I have been able to determine no coherent plan was ever developed within CIA to assassinate Castro, though it was the heart's desire of many exile groups." Even in the midst of planning an invasion, the CIA drew a line between subversion and assassination. Hunt, evidently, drew no such distinction.

Hunt has written that during the spring of 1960 he lunched one day with the invasion Project Director, "Jake," and Brigadier General Cushman (then military aide to Vice President Nixon), whom of course he knew from the days when they shared a CIA office in the 1950s. During lunch he reviewed for the General his impressions of Cuba under Castro and his principal recommendations, including the plan to assassinate Castro. Hunt, according to his account, went on to tell Cushman that his plan was to "form and guide the proposed Cuban government-in-exile, accompany its members to a liberated Havana, and stay on as a friendly adviser until after the first post-Castro elections." He was already casting himself in the role of the American pro-consul in Havana.

General Cushman, Hunt tells us, told him that Nixon was the

"action officer" for the invasion in the White House and wanted "nothing to go wrong." Cushman was therefore responsible for clearing bottlenecks and resolving differences among the State Department, the CIA, and the National Security Council. Cushman, according to Hunt, gave him his private telephone numbers and told him to call day or night whenever that might be required.

Give Us This Day is the title of Hunt's book on the Bay of Pigs invasion (it was published late in 1973, and the subtitle is *The Inside Story of the CIA and the Bay of Pigs Invasion—by One of Its Key Organizers.* One of the main themes running through this book is Hunt's bitterness over the fact that even the Eisenhower administration and its State Department favored relatively liberal elements in the Cuban exile community over Hunt's rightist protégés. "I came to understand that educated Cubans—professionals, industrialists, and ranchers—were to be allowed no role in building the new Cuba. At best they were 'reactionaries,' at worst 'Batisteros.' I realized that political vocabulary was outmoded; a new one was waiting for me to learn."

The Cuban exile Democratic Revolutionary Front, a CIA puppet group, initially operated from Mexico under Hunt's guidance. His first squabbles with the Cubans were over money. The Front wanted $750,000 a month from the CIA for all expenses, including infiltration and paramilitary work. But the Agency took the position that it alone would be responsible for this kind of expenditure. Hunt was authorized to pay the Front $115,000 a month, mostly for salaries and rentals of offices in the United States and Mexico. In Mexico City, Hunt operated independently from the local CIA station, though he used its communications system. Meanwhile, the CIA set up operational headquarters in Coral Gables, a suburb of Miami. An office there was converted for the use of the CIA and posed as an electronics firm engaged in government contracts. According to Hunt, this arrangement explained to any curious passers-by the building's tight guard system and massive installations of communication equipment. The Coral Gables operation was subsidizing exile groups as well as a number of newspapers formerly published in Havana that had now moved to the Miami area. This was part of a propaganda operation to sell subscriptions in Latin America at nominal cost to "spread the anti-Castro work in countries where Fidel was regarded sympathetically."

Hunt's personal favorite was the twenty-seven-year-old Manuel Artime, once a captain in Castro's army and chief of a land-reform sector in Oriente Province, who defected in 1959 and was ex-filtrated from Cuba by CIA. Hunt was pushing Artime for the command of the exile army that was beginning to undergo train-ing at secret camps in Guatemala. There, President Ydígoras Fuentes was repaying a 1954 debt to the United States. But Hunt was frustrated when the CIA refused freely to hand the Cuban leaders arms, explosives, and boats needed to engage in raids against Cuba. Instead, the Agency placed this responsibility in the hands of its paramilitary specialists. "Thus was my political mission undercut almost before it began," Hunt wrote later.

In Mexico City, Hunt set up a secret office in a small furnished house in the suburbs. He placed a large safe in the house and worked out operational schedules with his contacts at the local CIA station. It was in Mexico City too that Hunt first became aware of the existence of the man who was to become his *bête noire* during the preinvasion period. He was Manuel Ray, an engineer who had been chief of Castro's underground movement in Havana and later served as the first Minister of Public Works under the Revolution. Ray, however, became disenchanted with Castro and began building his own underground. Hunt, who held an instinctive dislike for most Cuban liberals, noted that Ray was often "described as a Marxist opportunist who had not rebelled against Castro when he forced Ray's brother, René, to kill himself following arrest for the alleged misappropriation of $400,000 seized by the revolution from the bank accounts of Cubans who had fled the country." Hunt claimed to have discovered that Ray "hated the landowning classes and saw a socialist solution for Cuba's post-Castro future." Here, obviously, was a man with whom Howard Hunt would not work.

The Mexican operation quickly became untenable because the Mexican police increasingly raided and kept under surveillance the CIA's "safe houses" and otherwise interfered in the conspiracy. Although the White House had originally stipulated that the Cuban project should not be carried out from American territory, it was nevertheless decided in the light of the situation in Mexico that the Cuban leadership—and Hunt—should be relocated in Miami. Now that Hunt undertook to operate clandestinely from Florida, it was not convenient for his family to be with him, so he dispatched Dorothy and the three children to Washington.

It was early October 1960 when Hunt set his Miami operation in motion. Invasion preparations were already well advanced. Men were being trained in Guatemala, while in Florida other CIA activities were in full swing. The Agency's procurement experts were searching the United States for rapid boats for infiltration raids into Cuba, and for old B-25 and B-26 bombers as well as C-46 transport planes to be used as part of a Guatemala-based rebel air force. The Cubans under Hunt's control had a recruiting office near Dinner Key, outside Miami. If approved by CIA in Washington (one of the considerations in approving the applications was to make sure that no former Batista followers were included in the brigade), the fighters were sent to Guatemala for training.

It is striking to see in what low esteem the CIA and Hunt held their Cuban clients. To be sure, the Cubans were continuously fighting among themselves; yet it probably would have made sense if they had been consulted to some degree as to how the operation against their own country should be run. But everything was centralized in the hands of the CIA. Cuban military officers in Miami were allowed to amuse themselves drafting invasion plans but, as Hunt said, these were not the plans that would be used. The real ones were being developed by the CIA and the Joint Chiefs of Staff at the Pentagon. To quote Hunt: "Cuban military planning, therefore, was a harmless exercise and might prove tangentially useful if they [sic] became known to Castro's agents and served as deception material—disinformation. To paraphrase a homily: this war was too important to be left to Cuban generals."

In Miami, Hunt acquired as his assistant a man who was fated to play another sadly fascinating role in American history a decade later. This was Bernard L. Barker, known as Bernie to Hunt and using the undercover name of "Macho," which means just that. Barker had an interesting history. He was born in the United States but lived in Cuba until World War II, when he joined the U.S. Army Air Corps and was shot down over Germany. After the war and his release from a prisoner-of-war camp, Barker went back to Havana, where the CIA convinced him to join the Cuban police so that the new Agency could have an operator inside the Cuban intelligence apparatus. This cost Barker his American citizenship. In 1960, before he fled Cuba for Miami, Barker arranged the escape of Captain Artime on the CIA's behalf. As Hunt remembered him in Miami in those early days, Barker was "eager, efficient and completely dedicated. Many days he was with me around the clock, and overall his help was invaluable." This was to be so again in 1971.

It is useful to note how in 1960 CIA funds for the Cuban exile operation were transmitted to Hunt from Washington to Miami through foreign banks. This was when the "laundering" of money through Miami was invented.

So active was Hunt in his little Miami apartment overlooking the Bay that all the comings and goings aroused the suspicions of neighbors and of the local police, who obviously knew nothing of his real purpose. In the end, it was necessary for him to move to a more discreetly located house in Coconut Grove, about a mile from the main CIA office in Miami. Operating under the new code name of "Eduardo"—a name that became famous ten years later—Hunt worked out of a house where, as he described it, "Plants and trees concealed [it] and screened the entrance, making it ideal for clandestine activity. Bernie found a Honduran cleaning woman, I rented office furniture, installed two telephones and was in business once again."

But the Cubans in Miami and Guatemala kept on fighting among themselves, and Hunt increasingly found himself in conflict with his CIA colleagues, especially the paramilitary people in charge of the training. Things reached the point where Hunt threatened to go personally to Allen Dulles with his complaints against the Agency's paramilitary personnel. Hunt felt that his political clients in the Cuban group were being ill-treated. There were other problems, too. Hunt's immediate neighbor and her daughter, a New York television model, soon concluded that Hunt was a homosexual because he was receiving so many male foreign visitors. Telling this episode, Hunt also relates that the divorced daughter, "a strikingly beautiful blonde," was brought down to Miami by her mother "to be very obviously shoved at me. . . ."

John F. Kennedy's election in November 1960 paralyzed the recruitment of the invasion force. The CIA was not quite sure how Kennedy felt about its secret plan. But Hunt, who claims to have met Kennedy in Boston many years earlier, was quickly reassured by his superiors that the halt was only temporary because Bissell was "well plugged into the Kennedy team" and operations could soon resume. Hunt made a point of noting in his memoirs that Bender, his immediate superior, had "a pro-Kennedy gleam in his eye." This was the sort of thing that made Hunt uncomfortable.

Sometime in November, Hunt attended a conference in Allen Dulles's office in Washington with General Charles P. Cabell (a Deputy Director), Bissell, Barnes, and a large number of military and CIA officers. One of the problems discussed was that the Cuban pilots flying supply missions for guerrilla groups in Cuba were inefficient. A Pentagon colonel suggested that American pilots and navigators be used, but Dulles vetoed this on the grounds that under White House rules, Americans were forbidden from entering Cuban air space. Then the group discussed specific invasion plans under which a Cuban government-in-exile, under Hunt's guidance, would be established on a beachhead in southern Cuba. From the beachhead, the scenario read, the exile leadership would appeal for international recognition, and the United States would, thereby, be given the necessary excuse to supply and reinforce the rebels. Hunt later made the point in his book that at no time were there plans for the Cuban underground to rise or play a decisive role in the campaign. Other senior CIA officers took that position, too, but the reality is that the Agency was hoping that insurgents inside the country would join up with the invaders. This is an important point, because the CIA has never wished to be accused of an intelligence failure at the Bay of Pigs, though it could live with a military defeat.

In December, word reached the CIA that a Cuban mission was purchasing fighter aircraft in the Soviet Union. Allen Dulles ruled that the invasion would have to occur before the Soviet aircraft could actually be delivered to the Cubans.

As the year 1961 began, the Cubans were fighting among themselves as never before. Hunt felt undercut, and, as he wrote, "I realized how far project emphasis had swung from political to military action." Pragmatically and ideologically, Hunt took the view that former Batista officers and soldiers should not be excluded from the invasion force because they were among the few available Cubans with military experience. He was "unwilling to sponsor guilt-by-association. . . ." (Everything else Hunt has said makes it clear that he felt more at home with the so-called

"Batisteros" than with more liberal Cubans such as Manuel Ray.)
As for the Cuban politicans in exile: ". . . I considered them shallow thinkers and opportunists who owed a large debt (their lives)
to the United States Government, and specifically to CIA. . . . if
not their leader, I was their guide, counselor, and *amicus curiae*."
Hunt had kind words only for Captain Artime. He thought him
to be as charismatic as Castro (a view shared by very few other
people) "fully aware that he owed us his life." Another factor in
Artime's favor was that he "believed profoundly that the Americans could do no wrong and that the way to free Cuba was to
cooperate with us, however devious and inexplicable our ways."
This, incidentally, was a philosophy that Hunt was to pursue ten
years later with the difference that "us" would then mean the
White House—"however devious and inexplicable our ways."

Meanwhile, Hunt was receiving blow after blow from CIA
headquarters. He bristled when the CIA ordered him to start
drafting a new Cuban constitution that would include clauses on
land reform, something that Castro had instituted immediately
after his revolution. Hunt argued against this in long telephone
discussions with Washington. But he was told that both Bissell
and Barnes had taken the view that *they* were the "real revolu-
tionaries" and that the rest of the United States government did
not even realize it. But one may agree with Hunt that Americans
had no business drafting a Cuban constitution, unless the United
States had wished to return to the relationships of Manifest
Destiny current at the turn of the century.

Some of the Cuban exile leaders believed that foreign investments in Cuba should be nationalized and the owners in-
demnified through long-term bonds. Shocked, Hunt responded
by emphasizing that American businessmen were contributing
heavily to the overthrow of Castro (a "fact" that was never officially confirmed) and that they would hardly welcome the idea
of supporting people committed to nationalization. Hunt argued
further that U.S. funds were not being spent for Cuban good will

alone but for assuring that the post-Castro regime would restore confiscated property to its rightful owners, whether Cuban or American. There he was, a right-wing ideologist, in the midst of a conspiracy to give Cubans a "better revolution." Hunt was also annoyed that one of Cuba's leading Roman Catholic priests, Monsignor Pérez Serantes (who interceded with Batista to save Castro's life after his aborted attack on an army barrack in Santiago in 1953), was not as anti-Castro as he should have been. Pérez Serantes "was under the sway of younger priests who were Castro partisans," and Hunt had visions of the French and Italian worker-priests whom he had learned to abhor in Europe.

In January 1961, diplomatic relations between the United States and Cuba were broken, with the result that the CIA station had to be moved out of Havana. Jim Noel, the Havana station chief, was assigned to the Miami operation, but Hunt considered his arrival to be "unwelcome" because "I felt him to be basically either soft on communism or at the least terribly confused about the isues." But what seemed to annoy Hunt the most was that Noel was a backer of Manuel Ray, whom Hunt could not tolerate politically. At this point, with pressures rising, Hunt was increasingly obsessive about the political coloration of the proposed invasion: he wanted to be sure it would be a rightist operation. He was resentful that Bender, his superior, had secretly visited Ray when Ray was brought to Tampa late in 1960 after the CIA helped him to escape. Hunt was so unhinged about Ray that he considered all of Ray's friends to belong to the "extreme Socialist Left." He also remarked that "Bender, who had a European Socialist background, took to them [Ray's associates] as a duck to water and revelled in the association. For my part I viewed Ray's group with maximum suspicion."

Hunt's views on the Cuban situation provide helpful clues to his philosophy and attitudes in assisting the Nixon White House many years later in carrying out its projects. It is worth quoting again from his book. Writing about these "extreme" socialists, Hunt said:

. . . they had tarried overlong to make their break with Castro's Communist regime and, safe on American shores, they proclaimed the doctrine (originally Trotsky's) of The Revolution Betrayed. This doctrine of theirs was eventually to permeate the highest levels of the U.S. government, finding welcome lodgement at the White House, the State Department, and CIA. Briefly, the thesis was that Castro's revolution had commenced on democratic lines and would have so continued had it not been for betrayal by Communists, among them Fidel Castro.

Similar theories, quite aside from Cuba, were often to be heard in Washington in the 1970s. Hunt himself transposed his thoughts about Cuban anti-Castro leftists to the American political scene. Remarking that a number of Kennedy's intimates were pro-Ray partisans, Hunt wrote that it seemed to him that "they all had a common background in Americans for Democratic Action—the ADA." (This, of course, is the left-wing Democratic political group in the United States.) Hunt was appalled that the Kennedy administration was favoring "the Democratic Left" in Latin America and that the new White House was proposing it "as a blueprint for Cuba's post-Castro future." Under Kennedy, Hunt noted, "our national tradition has become one of shabby discrimination against known anti-Communists." This obsesssive streak is the theme of Hunt's book, his "Political Testament." A novel Hunt wrote in the 1960s is a savagely transparent tale of knavery and ill-concealed softness on communism on the part of a Senator obviously modeled after the Kennedy brothers.

Hunt's only direct contact with the exile brigade that was to invade Cuba came when he made a visit to the training camps in Guatemala in the company of three members of the Executive Committee of the Democratic Revolutionary Front. One of them

was Artime, then undergoing special infiltration training at the
U. S. Army's school in the Panama Canal Zone. The purpose of
the trip was to meet with the Guatemalan president and then
go to the camps to quell what was quickly becoming a rebellion
by the troops against the Front. The underlying cause of tension
was that the Cuban civilian leadership wanted assurances that
there were no Batista supporters in the invasion force and that
the Miami group would form the core of a future Cuban government; brigade officers, on the other hand, were disturbed
by the politicians and insisted that only after "liberation" would
decisions be made as to who would run Cuba. Hunt, according
to his memoirs, played an important role in bringing the two
factions together. However, a group of "progressive" dissidents
were kept in virtual imprisonment in another part of Guatemala.
As matters stood shortly before the invasion, the brigade was
thus free of what Hunt would call socialist contagion.

After his visit to Guatemala, Hunt was back in Washington for
consultations with the CIA command. Again, bad news awaited
him. Bissell told him that he was under White House pressure
to include all possible elements of the Cuban exile groups in a
new Cuban Council, in whose name the invasion was to be
staged. Specifically, Bissell said, there was pressure for the inclusion of Manuel Ray. It was during this visit to Washington
that Hunt first set foot in the White House. He was taken there
by Barnes to meet Arthur M. Schlesinger, Jr., Assistant to President Kennedy, who was busy drafting a White Paper which was
to serve as the administration's political justification of the invasion. But Hunt did not have the opportunity to press his
divergent political views on Schlesinger.

Back in Miami, Hunt conferred with Dr. José Miró Cardona, a
law professor who had served for a month as Premier of the Revolutionary Government under Castro and then had fled Cuba for
Argentina, whence the CIA brought him to Miami. The latest
idea was to make Miró Cardona the head of the new Council.

Hunt found him to be cautious, politically sophisticated, and a man of "high integrity." Though Hunt convinced himself that Miró Cardona, though liberally inclined, could be useful to the operation, he kept struggling against Washington's proposals for Ray's inclusion in the new political organization. He wrote in his book that he argued that "to inject leftist ideology into the political front would destroy the Brigade, leaving the administration with exile leadership to its liking, but without a fighting force."

As the invasion approached, Hunt made a quick visit to Mexico to set up a new leadership for the local Cuban exile community, and then to Guatemala for a final conference with the local CIA station chief, Robert Davis. From there, he flew back to Washington on urgent instructions from the Agency. It was mid-March 1961. At a hard-eyed meeting at Bissell's office, overwhelming pressure was exerted on Hunt to accept Manuel Ray as a member of the Cuban Revolutionary Council. With a touch of desperation, Hunt insisted that Ray was proposing "Castroism without Fidel." He told his bosses that it was untrue that Ray controlled an underground movement in Cuba, as alleged. Ray was a "revisionist and an opportunist," and Hunt could not force the other members of the Council to accept him. But his objections were met with stunning silence from the senior CIA officers assembled in Bissell's office. They had their instructions from the White House. Hunt finally blurted out that he would rather withdraw from the operation than compromise on the issue. To his astonishment, no attempt was made to dissuade him from resigning. Jim Noel, the former Havana station chief whom Hunt so disliked and who was at the fateful conference, was named on the spot to replace him as the political mentor of the Cuban Council.

This marked the end of Howard Hunt's direct involvement with the Bay of Pigs invasion. He returned briefly to Miami to wind up his affairs, and only "Macho" Barker was on hand to commiserate with him. It was a strong friendship. But, as Hunt noted in his book, "it was becoming increasingly hard to identify the enemy."

Late in March, a gloomy Hunt flew home to Washington. The day before his return, his mother-in-law died at a Washington hospital after a long illness. In Hunt's life, disasters seem to come in clusters. Hunt now worked at CIA headquarters on propaganda related to the imminent landings. He kept in touch with the last-minute preparations, but he was obviously at the margin of the big operation. He was told, however, that once the beachhead at the Bay of Pigs was secured, he would be flown there to join what was hoped to be the new provisional government of Cuba.

On April 13, 1961, the invasion fleet left the Nicaraguan harbor of Puerto Cabezas and headed across the Caribbean toward the landing beaches in Cuba. On the morning of April 17, the brigade stormed ashore. Hunt, along with other CIA officers, monitored the unfolding events from the heavily guarded War Room on the first floor of Quarters Eye. It was there, during the seventy-two hours that the brigade fought on the beachhead before its men were killed or captured, that Hunt and his fellow CIA project officers listened to the dramatic radio messages announcing that the invading force had been smashed by Castro. They cursed Kennedy for refusing the brigade aid in the form of U. S. air cover.

In the aftermath of the Bay of Pigs invasion, the embittered Hunt was assigned to the office of Allen Dulles, the CIA's Director, to help set the record straight on the invasion. Kennedy had appointed a fact-finding body, known as the "Green Committee," with Colonel King as the principal staff officer, but to Hunt the whole purpose of the Presidential investigation was "to whitewash the New Frontier by heaping guilt on CIA." Hunt's job, as he described it, was to provide documentary and other material in reply to questions raised by the investigating committee's "inquisitors."

As a member of Dulles's staff, Hunt was also asked to assist the Director in the writing of his book *The Craft of Intelligence*. Someone had remembered that Hunt was a professional author, but a certain mystery still surrounds this literary cooperation between Dulles and Hunt. (I was told about it by a retired senior CIA official who was personally close to Dulles.) But after Hunt's involvement in Watergate became known, the CIA went out of its way to deny that Hunt had any part in the writing of the book. A spokesman insisted that the man who actually helped Dulles with the book was one Howard E. Roman, identified as a CIA official still on duty with the Agency. Roman does exist, but he could not be consulted about his role. Senior CIA officials have indicated privately that while Hunt did the actual literary work, Roman served as liaison with the publishing house.

Hunt was instructed at the same time to go over a long article in *Fortune* magazine about the Bay of Pigs—Dulles asked him to do so personally to assure its accuracy. Then Bissell assigned Hunt to represent the CIA on the Inter-Agency Committee on Cuba, which was studying what other measures could be taken against Castro. But Hunt found this work dull and unrewarding and asked to be assigned elsewhere. So Barnes shifted him to a non-Cuban project. In December 1962, after the Cuban missile crisis, Castro released the prisoners taken at the Bay of Pigs in exchange for an enormous shipment of medicine. Captain Artime was among those released, and he came to Washington to visit Hunt at his home, where they had an emotional meeting. This friendship, too, proved useful to Hunt in the year of Watergate.

Late in 1963, the CIA designated Howard Hunt to be the deputy station chief in Madrid. Officials say this was a reward for Hunt's assistance to Dulles in writing his book. It was generally known that Hunt liked Madrid, and his work there not only would be helpful to the Agency in terms of continuing Cuban operations, but would afford him an opportunity to go on writing.

But it was not to be so. As it happened, the American Ambassador in Madrid was Robert Woodward, and he had not forgotten Hunt's attempt to use the Uruguayan President and Eisenhower to avoid a transfer back to Washington in 1960. And, ironically, the CIA station chief was Jim Noel. Both Woodward and Noel, each for independent reasons, vetoed Hunt for the Madrid job. As far as it is known, this was the only time when the State Department actually opposed the appointment of a CIA officer to an embassy. Furthermore, the State Department asked the CIA to keep Hunt's name out of any future appointments to overseas diplomatic missions. Richard Helms, the new Director of the CIA replacing Dulles, fought hard for Hunt, but it was to no avail. The best that could be done for Hunt in 1963 was to assign him as acting chief of the CIA's Mexico City station during August and September.

Nevertheless, Hunt did go to Madrid sometime in 1964 for a stay that is believed to have lasted about two years. The reasons for his presence there remain unclear. Hunt made no effort to conceal his presence in Spain, because *Who's Who in America* in 1966 listed his home as Madrid and a literary agency in New York as his office address. It described him as a "retired government official," although he was still on the CIA payroll. Noel and other CIA officials who served in Madrid at the time insist that Hunt had no connections whatsoever with the local station. They tend to disbelieve a version, which I have reasons to consider reasonably accurate, that Hunt was secretly involved in a new Cuban enterprise.

This operation was intended to coordinate a second attempt

to invade Cuba, though on a smaller scale, with a plot to assassinate Castro. Directed by the CIA, the proposed invasion carried the code name of "Second Naval Guerrilla," and camps were established in Nicaragua and Costa Rica to train some 700 Cuban exiles. Some of the same CIA personnel that orchestrated the Bay of Pigs were involved in the new enterprise. One of them is believed to have been James McCord, a CIA security specialist who had played an ancillary role in the Bay of Pigs. McCord reportedly accepted the assignment when he returned from Europe, where he was the CIA's senior security officer. On the Cuban side, Captain Artime and Barker were involved. The idea, according to a number of men involved in the operation, was that a force led by Artime would land in Cuba around May 1965, after Castro was assassinated.

Hunt, according to the version with which I am familiar, was coordinating or helping to coordinate the assassination plot. It must be recalled that, according to his own memoirs, Hunt had strongly recommended Castro's assassination in 1960. In Madrid, Hunt is thought to have been in contact with Rolando Cubela, a former major in Castro's army. Because he had a scientific background, Cubela was allowed to travel freely to Paris and Madrid where, apparently, he made contact with the CIA. Artime was brought to Madrid in February 1964 for a secret meeting with Cubela. Subsequently, Cubela smuggled into Cuba an FAL automatic rifle outfitted with telescopic sights to kill Castro. It was given him by the CIA.

As part of the "second invasion" scheme, Hunt is also believed to have spent time in San José, the Costa Rican capital, checking on preparations in the camps in Central America. Some CIA sources say that he and Artime shared a "mansion" in downtown San José for a while. Charges have also been privately made that a C-46 cargo aircraft, attached to the operation, was sometimes used for smuggling from the Panama free zone to Costa Rica. But there is no proof of this.

The plot aborted when civil war broke out in the Dominican Republic in May 1965 and the Johnson administration did not consider it timely to mount another Caribbean operation after U. S. forces had invaded Santo Domingo. In 1966, Cubela was arrested by the Cuban secret police and sentenced to death after a brief trial. Castro commuted his sentence to life imprisonment. In announcing the plot, the Cubans named Jim Noel, the CIA's Madrid station chief, as the man who arranged the Cubela contacts. Noel denies having had any part in it. Hunt's name was never mentioned publicly in this context. But Hunt was known to only a very few people outside the Agency under his real name. Throughout the Bay of Pigs period, Cubans knew him only as "Eduardo."

In 1966, Hunt, now forty-eight years old, was beginning to consider retiring from the CIA. (The Hunt family was increased two years earlier with the birth of a fourth child, David.) The CIA was changing at a quick pace, and it increasingly emphasized new intelligence technology at the expense of traditional covert work, for which there seemed to be less and less need. In the words of a senior Agency official, Hunt was considered as a "burned out" case officer. After 1966, he was given generally irrelevant jobs, and it was made clear to him that he could expect no further advancement. He held the relatively high GS-15 Civil Service grade which paid him more than $20,000 a year, but he was feeling the pressure to take early retirement.

During 1967, he wrote his book on the Bay of Pigs, *Give Us This Day*. It is a bitter book. "Castro's beachhead triumph opened a bottomless Pandora's box of difficulties that affected not only the United States, but most of its allies in the Free World," Hunt wrote. Like so many men identified with Cuban causes, Hunt came to regard the Caribbean island as a major center of international politics—a concept unreal in this age, when one thinks of Nixon going to Peking and Moscow. Even Hunt's visceral anticommunism had become obsolete.

In a bizarre passage in the book's foreword, written early in 1973, Hunt speaks of Kennedy's assassination. Then he makes this comment: "Once again it became fashionable to hold the city of Dallas collectively responsible for his murder. Still, and let this not be forgotten, Lee Harvey Oswald was a partisan of Fidel Castro, and an admitted Marxist who made desperate efforts to join the Red Revolution in Havana. In the end, he was an activist for the Fair Play for Cuba Committee. "But for Castro and the Bay of Pigs disaster there would have been no such 'Committee.' And perhaps no assassin named Lee Harvey Oswald."

As I mentioned above, Hunt spent August and September 1963 in Mexico City in charge of the CIA station there. Through an extraordinary coincidence, Lee Harvey Oswald also visited Mexico City during September 1963.

Hunt had no plans to publish his book at the time it was written. For one thing, he was still employed by the CIA. But after the eruption of the Watergate scandal and as his trial approached early in 1973, Hunt decided to unveil his account of the Bay of Pigs. "In 1972 . . . my name was blazoned across the country in connection with the Watergate affair, and government sources revealed to the press the fact that I had been a CIA official. Moreover, these same sources provided the press with distorted accounts of my involvement in the Bay of Pigs invasion.

"This unilateral action by the government relieved me of the obligation to maintain further secrecy concerning my CIA connection and the true role that I and others played in the Cuba Project."

In his own way, Hunt was breaking forever with the CIA, and before too long he turned on it.

In 1968, the Hunts came back to Washington and bought a property, curiously named Witches' Island, in Potomac, a fashionable Maryland suburb of Washington in the heart of the horse country. Dorothy Hunt was a dedicated horsewoman, and this may have been among the reasons why they picked Potomac for their new home. The cost of Witches' Island has been reported to have been $200,000, but this is probably an exaggerated estimate. Even with income from books and his CIA salary, the chances are that Hunt could not have afforded that much for a home. And he always seemed to be in financial difficulties.

Howard Hunt spent nearly two years working at the CIA's gleaming new headquarters in Langley, Virginia. His final secret mission—still undisclosed—was in late 1968, when he turned up in Paris inexplicably adorned with a full-grown beard. At poker games with friends, he flashed brand-new $100 bills. Apparently, the CIA chooses to supply its agents with money in this fashion. In Washington, the Hunts were quite sociable in those days. Several of his colleagues remember attending cocktail parties that Hunt would throw to mark the retirement of other fellow workers from the Agency. On April 30, 1970, Hunt himself retired from the CIA after nearly twenty-three years of service.

THE DEED

1

Howard Hunt is not a man who believes in retirement or vacations. In the afternoon of April 30, 1970, he walked out for the last time from the headquarters of the Central Intelligence Agency. Next morning, May 1, he was at work at his new job with the Robert R. Mullen & Company public relations firm, on Pennsylvania Avenue in downtown Washington.

Hunt was fifty-one years old going on fifty-two, and he desperately wanted and needed employment. His constant need for money was something of a mystery to his friends and associates. His CIA pension was $24,000 and the Mullen company was paying him $24,000 a year. Dorothy, his wife, worked part time at the Spanish Embassy, where she wrote letters in English for the Ambassador. The family's income, therefore, had to be at least $50,000, which was not bad in Washington in 1970. Besides, Hunt received residual royalties from some of the forty-four novels he had published over the previous twenty-eight years.

To be sure, the family had high expenses and they lived well. The mortgage and upkeep for Witches' Island was rather high. Kevan, the younger daughter, was attending Smith college. Lisa, the eldest, had a history of illness, and medical bills must have been considerable. Earlier, both girls had attended Holton Arms, an expensive private girls' school in the Maryland suburbs not far from the Hunts' house. The family had two cars, a Chevrolet and a Pontiac. Kevan had a red Opel station wagon of her own.

The Hunts lived comfortably, then. On Howard's insistence, they dined every evening by candlelight. They were busy on the suburban Potomac cocktail circuit. Their house was full of animals—cats and dogs and birds and even, once, a small boa constrictor. By all accounts, Dorothy was a warm and loving mother to her children. She was interested in Howard's new activities. Now that he had left the CIA, he could talk freely about his work—at least for a while. Friends who visited the Hunts during weekends found them relaxed and at ease. Howard, puffing on his pipe, would fondle one of the kittens. Dorothy mixed the drinks. Much of the housework was done by a Uruguayan woman who had been with the Hunts since their days in Montevideo more than ten years earlier. All in all, it was a rather pleasing picture of a well-to-do American family, with the father embarked on a new career, the mother working but dedicated to the children and to her pursuit of horsemanship, and the kids doing well at school.

Yet things were not all that simple downtown for Howard Hunt. In the first place, he was frustrated in his job. In the second place, he craved more money. The frustration evidently came from the instant transition from a glamorous association with the CIA (so it was believed to be) to the brain-addling dullness of writing press releases and other publicity material for the Mullen firm. For this is what Hunt was doing at 1700 Pennsylvania Avenue, although he claimed he was a vice president of the company. As Richard Helms was to testify in the summer of 1973 at the Senate Select Committee hearings, Hunt had been given undemanding jobs at the Agency in his last two years because of his daughter's medical problems, which, Helms said, required much of his attention. Still, it was painful for Hunt to be cut off so abruptly from the CIA and from the comforting sense of belonging to an elite, even though Hunt was increasingly critical of the CIA for losing its old aplomb. Now he was an outsider in the intelligence community and a "has-been." It must have rankled. Humorously or wistfully, Hunt decorated his personal memo pad, the kind that has the owner's name at the top, with an imprinted "00?" in the right-hand corner. This play on James Bond's "007" code number, which indicated "license to kill," revealed Hunt's uncertainty over his own identity in the context of a new life.

Financially, Hunt was always "haggling" for more money, as his associates at the public-relations company reported later. When he first discussed joining the Mullen firm before his retirement

from the CIA, he talked about buying into the company. Robert
Rodolf Mullen, founder and chairman of the board, was in his
sixties and thinking about retirement. Hunt expressed an interest
in buying a share of his equity, but when the time came he
seemed to have difficulties in raising the $2000 in "earnest
money" which the Mullen firm required. Later, he put up an
argument for an $8000 salary increase—this would have brought
up his salary to $32,000—but the Mullen people turned him down.
Hunt made noises about resigning over the money issue but never
did anything about it.

Actually, the Mullen company was an interesting place for a
man like Hunt to be in Washington in 1970. Robert Mullen, a
veteran newspaper man, had served as director of public information for the Economic Corporation Administration between 1946
and 1948 (the latter being the year when Howard Hunt used
the ECA as his CIA cover in the Paris station). It is unclear
whether Mullen and Hunt met in those days, although it is possible that Mullen had some contacts with the Agency. In any
event, the two references Hunt gave when he applied for the job
with the Mullen company were Richard Helms and William F.
Buckley, Jr. Helms was then still Director of the CIA and
Buckley, an old CIA friend, was now a famous commentator.
Many people around Washington believe that there is indeed
such a thing as a CIA "old-boy network."

At the time of the Watergate raid and in subsequent testimony
before the Senate Investigating Committee, Helms insisted that
he barely knew Hunt. But there are reasons to believe that Helms
was at least quite aware of Hunt's existence. For one thing, according to senior Agency officials, Helms tried hard to get Hunt
the Madrid station job which Allen Dulles had promised him. For
another thing, Helms kept copies of Hunt's spy novels around
his office and often gave or lent them to friends and visitors.

As for the Mullen firm, it was extremely close to Republican
power in Washington. The firm's president—and the man who

really ran it—was Robert F. Bennett, the son of the Republican Senator from Utah. Bob Bennett, an affable but strict Mormon, came to the firm from the Department of Transportation where, in 1969, he was the White House's unofficial representative in the office of John A. Volpe, then Transportation Secretary. (This was the pattern of the Nixon administration from the very outset. In every department of government there was a trusted White House person who made sure that the Presidential staff were fully informed about what went on at all times.)

Bennett was very well acquainted around Washington, and the firm held some valuable accounts. One of them was to represent in Washington the interests of Howard Hughes, the elusive billionaire. This was rather more a political than a public-relations job; it meant that Hughes received reports from the Mullen firm on the political situation in Washington. Bob Bennett also looked after such things as Hughes's contributions to the Republican campaign. Another important account was General Foods. Then there was the Department of Health, Education and Welfare—an account that Bennett assigned to Hunt when he joined the firm. Earlier, Bennett had helped to set up Republican finance committees around the country and, in 1971, he was engaged in the successful effort by the milk producers' lobby to win a higher price support from the Agriculture Department. The milk men gave the Nixon campaign more than $300,000.

In terms of Washington's political geography, the Mullen firm was most conveniently located. It was a block away from the White House on Pennsylvania Avenue, and across the street from the building which in March 1971 would house the headquarters of the Committee to Re-Elect the President. (The Committee's building was called simply "1701"—this was its street number—when Presidential politics went into full swing. Nixon's former law firm had offices there, too.)

But Howard Hunt was being kept down, and he resented it. Bob Bennett is said to have thought highly of Hunt as a writer of publicity material, but he had doubts about Howard's capacity to handle "outside" contacts with important clients. At one point, Hunt tried to assume responsibility for the Hughes account but in this, too, he was disappointed. The day the word came that Hughes had flown from his hideaway in Nassau to Managua, Nicaragua, Hunt burst into Bennett's office to say that he knew the Nicaraguan President, Tachito Somoza, quite well from his CIA days. Surely he could help Hughes in Managua? The Mullen people thought this was rather amusing; about the last thing in the world Howard Hughes needed was help from Howard Hunt. Hughes had bought equity in Nicaraguan Airlines, which was one way of doing business with Somoza, and he had plans for other considerable investments in the little Central American Republic.

Hunt also turned out to be something of a social climber. He was a member of the Army and Navy Club, a respectable conservative institution, and of the less known Tavern Inn Club. But he was anxious to be a member of the *very* prestigious Metropolitan Club in Washington, and he kept pressing Bennett and other friends, who belonged to it, to put him up for membership. He was a bit of a snob, too, and there is a story that on one social occasion he cut a woman he met dead, until he discovered that she was a graduate of one of the expensive New England girls' colleges. Status is what counts in Washington— whether one is a politician, public figure, or businessman.

And he was always acting the debonair Washingtonian. He liked to date pretty women (which he did with varying degrees of success), and those who were exposed to his company in such circumstances suggested that listening to Hunt was a bit like reading his Paris novels. He often patronized the Blues Alley, a fairly fashionable Georgetown establishment, where one could get lunch or dinner. Or he went to the Potomack, a Georgetown restaurant specializing in early American food and décor (unfortunately, it has since gone out of business). People who knew him said that Hunt had always maintained his old penchant for good food and fine beverages. State Department friends recall an incident at Christmastime in 1960, when Hunt was involved in the Cuban invasion project but came to Washington for the holidays. Having drunk too much, they said, he displayed all his fake CIA identity papers—in those days he used the cover name of "Eduardo"—and this, of course, was a major breach of security. Ten years later, in 1970, Hunt's tastes and inclinations had not much changed.

While Hunt was occupied during the spring and summer of 1970 with his professional and personal frustrations, President Nixon was increasingly concerned with political "law and order" in the country and his staff was preparing to launch its top-secret domestic intelligence plan. This White House activity was presumably unknown to Hunt as he slaved away at his typewriter at 1700 Pennsylvania Avenue, but it was to become enormously relevant before too long that one of the White House inner sanctum planners was a cordial friend of the embittered former intelligence operative.

This friend was Charles W. Colson, Special Counsel to the President, and one of the most powerful (some people said one of the most ruthless) men in Nixon's White House. Colson, a fat, bespectacled man and former Marine combat officer, was like Hunt a Brown University alumnus. They had met around 1966 at a function at the Washington chapter of the Brown University Alumni Association (both were officers of the association), and apparently they hit it off right away. They maintained pleasant relations in ensuing years, and after Hunt left the CIA he began to court Colson with considerable assiduity. Hunt understood power, and he knew where it was centered in Washington. To him, Colson could be an entree to the power circles of the administration. The Hunts and the Colsons lived fairly near each other. On occasion, they met for family dinners and spent some hours during weekends when the Special Counsel was not too busy downtown. It was not an intimate friendship—Colson tended to look down on Hunt—but Hunt made it appear that they were extremely close to each other, and he made the most of it. Bob Bennett was also acquainted with Colson, and the three men met to chat about Republican politics.

The state of Republican and, for that matter, Presidential politics was not particularly encouraging in the summer of 1970. Abroad, the Vietnam war was dragging on without any prospect of either victory or settlement, although Henry Kissinger had for nearly a year been conducting desultory secret meetings with the North Vietnamese in Paris. At home, protest against the war had reached violent proportions. Students had been killed at Kent and Jackson State universities during demonstrations against the American invasion of Cambodia in May. During the autumn of 1969, the first great antiwar Moratorium had been held in Washington, with hundreds of thousands of people on hand to protest; and the antiwar movement was acquiring political dimensions of its own. The men in the White House began suspecting that some sort of sinister conspiracy was under way to damage or destroy the constituted government of the United States. John Mitchell, then Attorney General, compared the surging crowds of antiwar protesters to the Bolshevik revolution. The Justice Department and the FBI provided the White House with daily reports on bombings, arson, and other violence perpetrated by young people against military and other government installations. In 1969 and 1970, there were 1800 demonstrations in the country and four hundred and forty colleges went on strike over the Cambodian invasion. The little knot of men in the White House had visions of groups like the Weathermen faction of Students for Democratic Society and the Black Panthers becoming the spearhead of a Castro-like guerrilla operation in the United States. The White House was evidently losing its sense of proportion in judging American society.

Other foreign situations worried the White House. In June 1970, the top-secret 40 Committee met to decide what if anything should be done if Salvador Allende Gossens, a Socialist, were elected President of Chile in the approaching September elections. As far as it is known, the only decision was that the CIA, working with its normal operational funds, would subsidize anti-Allende media in Chile. In September, after Allende's election, the 40 Committee met again at the White House to review the Chilean situation. This was around the time when the International Telephone and Telegraph Corporation incredibly offered the CIA the sum of $1 million to prevent Allende's inauguration. No decision was taken for any serious action in Chile.

Nonetheless, Kissinger was setting a tone for the administration's over-all political attitude toward Chile when he told newsmen at a background meeting in Chicago that Allende's triumph raised the threat of Communist take-overs in other South American countries such as Argentina, Uruguay, and Brazil. The United States was also going through a mini-crisis with the Soviet Union over the administration's suspicions that the Russians were preparing to establish refueling and other facilities in Cuba for long-range nuclear submarines.

These disturbing internal and external problems aside, the White House had already been engaged for a year in secret activities against its political opponents. As early as 1969, the White House quietly hired two special investigators to look into alleged wrongdoings by Democrats and other groups opposing Nixon policies. They were Anthony I. Ulasewicz and John Caul-

field, both retired New York City policemen. John D. Ehrlichman, then Nixon's Domestic Affairs Adviser, acknowledged before the Senate Investigating Committee that he had a role in
hiring Ulasewicz for the purpose of gathering information about
the sex life, drinking habits, and domestic relations of the political
opponents of the President. Ulasewicz himself spelled it out in
breath-taking detail before the Senate panel. (In late July 1969
Ulasewicz was instructed to investigate the accident on Chappaquiddick Island when Mary Jo Kopechne drowned in a car
driven by Senator Edward M. Kennedy. Ulasewicz also told the
committee that he had been investigating other Senators, as well
as financial contributions to Senator Edmund Muskie, then the
front-running Democratic candidate.)

Interestingly, both Ehrlichman and Ulasewicz defended these
investigations as a perfectly proper form of political activity. The
whole thing was a question of philosophy and mentality. We can
see, of course, that Ehrlichman, the powerful adviser to President
Nixon, and Tony Ulasewicz, the double-chinned former cop,
operated on the same ethical assumptions (or nonassumptions) as
Howard Hunt had done for a good part of his life in foreign
intelligence. The ethical environment prevailing in the White
House was, therefore, excellently adapted to Hunt's own conviction that any actions conducted under the auspices of "proper
authority" were valid. It was only a question of time before Hunt
would naturally gravitate to the White House orbit.

When autumn 1970 came, the White House was gravely dis-
turbed over the political picture on the eve of mid-term elections.
Because Alabama's maverick Democratic Governor, George C.
Wallace, loomed as a threat to the Republicans' "Southern
Strategy," the White House secretly arranged to provide $400,000
from surplus 1968 Nixon campaign funds to Wallace's opponent.
In October, Nixon ran into rock-hurling demonstrators in San
Jose, California. This really pushed the White House to believe
that there was some sort of a conspiracy against the President.

The Democrats' strong showing in the November elections, following an impressive last-minute speech by Muskie, further deepened the White House concern that Nixon might be facing serious trouble in his hoped-for bid for re-election.

As we have seen earlier, J. Edgar Hoover had succeeded in July 1970 in blocking the admittedly illegal domestic intelligence plan drafted by the young White House aide Tom Huston. Nixon was to say later that the plan was rescinded a few days after its approval (this reversal cost Huston his intelligence niche in the White House), but the idea did not die there. In December 1970, when the White House had recovered from the shock of the mid-term elections, Nixon authorized the creation of a top-secret Intelligence Evaluation Committee made up of representatives from the Presidential staff, FBI, CIA, NSA, the Secret Service, and the Departments of Defense, Treasury, and Justice.

It is unclear whether Hoover was informed about the IEC, but it is significant that it was fitted into the Internal Security Division in the Justice Department. The Division reported directly, and independently of the FBI, to the Attorney General, who, in turn, kept Nixon informed. As the President explained later, the IEC was "instructed to improve coordination among the intelligence community and to prepare evaluations and estimates of domestic intelligence." One of the IEC's assignments was to predict the scope of demonstrations and the likelihood of violence at them. The new committee had no operational responsibilities, but its members included a representative of the CIA, whose charter prohibits domestic operations, along with the military intelligence agencies, whose normal function is to worry about foreign enemies. (There was the precedent here of the Army's Counter-Intelligence Division, which spied on members of Congress and political activists as far back as 1968, and set up its intelligence data bank on thousands of civilians.)

In any event, the IEC was the forerunner of the Special Investigative Unit, an operational group that grew in the greatest secrecy in the White House the next year, and that set in motion the "White House horrors" with the active participation of E. Howard Hunt.

Even before Hunt joined the White House staff in mid-July 1971, he and the public-relations firm where he worked were already well involved with the Presidential offices. For one thing, there was the relationship among Hunt, Colson, and Bob Bennett. Business was of course discussed when the three met, and the fact that the Mullen company held a Howard Hughes account turned out to be of intense interest to the White House.

On January 5, 1971, for example, Colson wrote a confidential memorandum to Roy Goodearle, then an aide to Vice President Agnew, recommending that Bennett be introduced to Agnew in order to "enhance" his influence in Washington. Colson's memo said that "Bob is a trusted loyalist and a good friend. We intend to use him on a variety of outside projects. One of Bob's (new) clients is Howard Hughes. I am sure I need not explain the political implications of having Hughes' affairs handled here in Washington by a close friend." Colson went on to emphasize that "this move could signal quite a shift in terms of the politics and money that Hughes represents. Bob Bennett tells me that he has never met the Vice President, and that it would enhance his position greatly if we could find an appropriate occasion for him to come in and spend a little time talking with the Vice President. The important thing from our standpoint is to enhance Bennett's position with Hughes because Bennett gives us real access to a sort of power that can be valuable, and it's in our interest to build him up."

Hunt, as noted earlier, had wanted badly to handle the Hughes account in the Mullen firm. He must have realized that this would have brought him even closer to the White House power center. But Bennett preferred to keep the account in his own hands, although as it turned out he never met Agnew because the Vice President canceled a scheduled meeting. Hughes's contribution to the 1972 Nixon campaign was $200,000, but there are no indications that any special relationship had developed between the recluse billionaire and the White House, despite Colson's anxious hopes.

There was an ironic ending to this Hughes story. In June 1971, the White House discovered that Lawrence F. O'Brien's public-relations firm (O'Brien was Chairman of the Democratic National Committee) also had an annual retainer from Hughes, who evidently likes to spread his business around. On June 28, H. R. Haldeman, the President's chief of staff, wrote a confidential memo to John W. Dean III, counsel to the President, that "you and Chuck Colson should get together and come up with a way to leak the appropriate information [about O'Brien's retainer from Hughes]." (Haldeman failed to explain why such information would be detrimental to O'Brien, but his memo shows that the White House had nothing against news leaks so long as they came from Nixon's own staff as part of deliberate strategy.) He wrote that the information had come from Bob Bennett, who had the other Hughes account in Washington, and Charles G. (Bebe) Rebozo, the President's closest personal friend. "We should keep Bob Bennett and Bebe out of it all," he added. Haldeman was obviously unaware that Caufield, the White House secret investigator, had recommended to Dean almost five months earlier that the O'Brien-Hughes story should *not* be leaked out because a "forced embarrassment of O'Brien in this matter might shake loose the Republican skeletons from the closet."

Caulfield, who clearly does *his* homework, had added the fascinating bit of news that "Don Nixon [the President's brother] visited the Dominican Republic with a group of wheeler-dealers in September, 1969, who assertedly were connected with the Hughes interests." Donald Nixon's trip to Santo Domingo was made from Reno, Nevada, aboard a private jet belonging to a Hughes associate. My own understanding is, by the way, that the "wheeler-dealers" were interested in a casino gambling franchise in the Dominican Republic. They were received along with Don Nixon by the Dominican President, Joaquín Balaguer, whose own interest was to obtain a bigger sugar quota in the United States. But Caulfield obviously was also remembering that Hughes had made a controversial loan to the Nixon brothers back in 1952. He evidently feared that embarrassing O'Brien might raise again the story of that old loan.

Another incident concerning the White House, the Mullen firm, and Hunt occurred in 1972, after Howard Hunt already was an undercover agent for the Presidency. The HEW account held by the Mullen firm included publicity work for a program for handicapped children. Hunt used his White House connections to persuade Julie Eisenhower, the President's daughter, to tape a television spot on behalf of this program. Bennett decided, however, that Julie's appearance on television during an election year might be misinterpreted politically, and he told Hunt that the spot should be held back until after November. Hunt hit the roof. He went to the White House, and the next day he informed Bennett that it was the President's personal wish that Julie's tape be used as soon as possible. Bennett, who often had his doubts about the accuracy of Hunt's statements, stood his ground, and the spot was not broadcast until after the elections.

On June 13, 1971, *The New York Times* published the first installment of the Pentagon Papers, dealing with the past conduct of the Vietnam war in the Kennedy and Johnson administrations. Nixon was horrified by what he regarded as a security leak of monumental proportions. He took the view that urgent measures were required not only to prevent continued publication in the *Times* of the government papers, but also to start plugging other leaks in the government. For this reason, as White House witnesses were to tell the story before the Senate Investigating Committee, a decision was made to establish in the White House a Special Investigative Unit to make sure that there would be no further breaches of security. But beginning in 1969, the President and Kissinger had authorized the wiretapping of telephones of a number of White House and National Security Council aides, apparently to make sure that they were not leaking information to the press. Home telephones of several Washington newspapermen were also tapped. So the important thing was that the Pentagon Papers provided the rationalization for organizing the Special Unit, something that the White House had desired ever since Tom Huston drafted his domestic intelligence plan. The unit was established in the first days of July 1971 in total secrecy.

As the story was to unfold in public testimony before the Senate Select Committee during the summer of 1973, Nixon asked John Ehrlichman to act as the over-all supervisor of the Special Investigative Unit. Egil Krogh, Jr., a member of the White House Domestic Council, was the man who actually put the secret unit together. David R. Young, Jr., came from the National Security Council to act as co-chairman. Krogh and Young, in turn, decided to draft Howard Hunt and G. Gordon Liddy, an aggressive and colorful White House staffer with an FBI background, to serve as the unit's chief operatives.

In his testimony, Ehrlichman described the function of the unit, which became known as "the plumbers": "The Unit as originally conceived was to stimulate the various departments and agencies to do a better job of controlling leaks and the theft or other exposure of national security secrets from within their departments. It was a group which was to bring to account, so to speak, various security officers of the Department of Defense and State and Justice and CIA, to get them to do a better job." Ehrlichman testified that in addition to the Pentagon Papers, the President was concerned about other current news leaks, particularly articles in *The New York Times* disclosing the U. S. negotiating position in the Strategic Arms Limitation Talks with the Soviet Union and summarizing a CIA report on relations between India and Russia. (I happened to be the author of the India story and, as I found out later, my telephone, too, was tapped by the Special Unit.)

There is also talk that the plumbers were engaged in investigating the international traffic in narcotics, and this in part may be true. But the most important and rather terrifying aspect of the unit's known operations was that the White House subsequently invoked "national security" at every turn to justify the unit—a private secret-police detachment formed by political fanatics—and its deeds. Yet the record, incomplete as it clearly remains, shows no actions that could be reasonably construed as being related to national security in its generally accepted sense. The break-in at the office of Daniel Ellsberg's psychiatrist to obtain hoped-for files from which the CIA could construct his psychological profile, or Hunt's and Liddy's involvement in the secret dealings between the Nixon administration and ITT strain the imagination when they are portrayed officially as "national-security operations."

Nixon himself provided an intriguing insight into the labors of the unit when he said in a formal statement on Watergate on August 15, 1973, that upon learning of the Ellsberg raid, almost twenty-one months after it occurred, and of the Justice Department's plans to interrogate Hunt, he became "gravely concerned that other activities of the Special Investigative Unit might be disclosed, because I knew this could seriously injure the national security." Aside from the Ellsberg and ITT situations, the Watergate burglaries, and a few other acts of political espionage and sabotage performed by Hunt and his associates, we do not know what else the secret unit may have done. The President seemed to suggest that there were still other and thus far undisclosed operations conducted by Hunt's team. Inasmuch as the White House has a highly flexible concept of what constitutes national security, Nixon's statement leaves us with still another mystery.

During those summer months of 1971, the White House was evidently obsessed by suspicions of great conspiracies. Although the violence of 1969 and 1970 had subsided, the administration reacted with near hysteria when antiwar radicals attempted to close down the city of Washington on May Day 1971, by blocking access roads into the capital and the principal thoroughfares. The Army was brought out to guard the bridges and their approaches, and by the end of the day Metropolitan Police had arrested over 12,000 persons—unquestionably a national record and another "first" for the Nixon administration—although it was subsequently unable to have the courts accept the charges against the demonstrators.

On another level, as Ehrlichman testified, great concern was shown over information obtained by the White House that a set of the Pentagon Papers had allegedly been turned over to the Soviet Embassy. Ehrlichman said that he knew about this "because I had a call from . . . the Assistant Attorney General, advising me that the Justice Department had this for a fact. The Attorney General came over and reported to the President that this theft had evidently been perpetrated by a number of people, a conspiracy, that some of the people had been identified by the Department of Justice as having had previous ties to domestic Communist activities." But the White House has never produced evidence of any kind that the Pentagon Papers had actually been made available to the Soviet Embassy before their publication in *The New York Times* or that Daniel Ellsberg or anyone assisting him had past Communist ties.

Ehrlichman also testified that he and his associates were convinced that the FBI would not investigate Ellsberg and his associates and that, therefore, it was necessary for the Presidential staff to take matters into its own hands. This was how the White House launched its private secret police operations.

Howard Hunt was hired for the Special Unit on July 6, 1971, in the role of consultant to the White House. The man who recommended him for the job was his friend Chuck Colson. During his testimony before the Senate Committee, Ehrlichman was asked whether "it be fair to say that Mr. Colson very much wanted Mr. Hunt to be hired?" Ehrlichman answered: "That would be fair to say." Hunt retained his job at the Mullen company, however (it was, among other things, a fine intelligence cover), and he was paid $130 a day in consultant fees for each day he worked for the White House. The money came from a $1.5-million White House Special Project Fund—from which Tom Huston, author of the original intelligence plan, was also paid.

Under government regulations, Hunt was not supposed to be paid by the White House because he was receiving a CIA pension. The law provides that a person may not be paid at the same time by two different government agencies. But since the White House project was a secret one, this legal requirement made no difference. Hunt did actually raise the issue with Colson, who, in turn, contacted Ehrlichman. According to White House staffers, Ehrlichman ruled that it was "OK" to pay Hunt his consultant's fee along with expenses.

The plumbers set up shop in Room 16 of the Executive Office Building, on the ground floor, separated from the White House by the narrow West Executive alley. The building is part of the White House complex. Hunt also had additional space for his own use in a suite assigned to Colson on the third floor. The Special Unit was known as "Room 16 Project." Such was the secrecy surrounding the operation that a special telephone in Room 16 was listed under the name of Kathy Chenow, a White House secretary, instead of its being just another government number, and the bills were sent to her home. This was Hunt's idea. David Young's National Security Council office phone number was also available to the plumbers.

It is important to establish the distinction, subtle as it may seem, between the operations of the Special Unit as such and the subsequent activities by Hunt, Liddy, and their hell-raising teams. The Special Unit functioned formally only between July and late September 1971. After that, Hunt joined the political espionage and sabotage operation known as Project Gemstone, devised by Liddy and financed by the Committee to Re-Elect the President. But he remained on the White House payroll until March 1972 and maintained his office until the Watergate break-in on the night of June 17/18,1972, and never severed his White House ties.

The distinction is interesting because this arrangement later gave the White House the opportunity to claim that crimes committed after the Special Unit was theoretically dissolved should be laid at the door of the Committee to Re-Elect the President. The White House wanted the best of both worlds: it wanted the operations conducted by Hunt to go on, but it wished to be able to disassociate itself from them if necessary. It was both duality and duplicity.

This duplicity was so great that at one point in 1972, the White House "borrowed" Hunt (Liddy had moved over to the Re-Election Committee in February 1972) to cover up an unpleasantness that had resulted from a compromising memorandum written by a former ITT lobbyist who had tied the Republican party to an antitrust suit against the huge corporation. And the plumbers were summoned again after the syndicated columnist, Jack Anderson, published top-secret memos from a National Security Council meeting concerning the Indo-Pakistani war in December 1971. But they never discovered Jack Anderson's source.

Howard Hunt was overjoyed, to put it mildly, when the White House recruited him for its secret operations. All of a sudden, the boredom and frustration were left behind and now Hunt was back in his beloved role as an undercover intelligence operative. And this was even better than the CIA: it was clandestine work under the direct authority of the President of the United States to save the nation from its domestic foes.

Hunt also enjoyed his personal relationship with Gordon Liddy, an off-beat type after his own heart. A one-time FBI agent and assistant district attorney in New York State, Liddy was something of a buccaneer, and Hunt appreciated that. Frances Liddy, his wife and the mother of his five children, was to write later that after they moved to Washington, "Hunt and his late wife were the only ones we ever saw socially." Hunt "seemed to find Gordon fascinating. . . . I wonder now if Hunt, consciously or unconsciously, was intending to make Gordon a character in a future book. . . . I remember one story that amused Hunt. Gordon had led a narcotics raid on Dr. Timothy Leary's house. The air was so full of marijuana smoke that the family's dog was out cold. When Gordon burst into the living room, the pooch was lying on his back, all four paws rigid in the air."

We do not know how much Colson, Krogh, Young, or indeed Liddy, told Hunt about the ultimate purpose of the Special Unit. Ehrlichman has testified that he met Hunt only once—after Colson arranged for Hunt to be hired, and Hunt naturally did not question the motives. But there he was, under the auspices of the nation's "highest authority," and clearly he had no ethical scruples about what he was being asked to do. The important thing was that he was in business again, back practicing the craft of intelligence and, for the first time in his life, really rubbing elbows with the most powerful men of the realm.

Much of what ensued after Hunt came aboard at the White House is still a matter of murky controversy among administration witnesses who have testified before the Senate Committee and other Congressional panels.

General Cushman, Commandant of the Marine Corps, who served as Deputy Director of the CIA in 1971, claimed in his testimony that Ehrlichman called him on July 7, 1971—one day after Hunt was hired by the White House—to ask him to provide the latter with necessary assistance in the fulfillment of a national-security mission. Although Ehrlichman testified that he could not recall "ever making such a call," Cushman went to Capitol Hill well armed with a total recall of the events and with transcripts of a tape recording of his conversation with Hunt at CIA head-quarters.

General Cushman testified that when Ehrlichman called him about Hunt, he assumed that this was being done on Nixon's behalf:

I knew that he . . . spoke with the authority of the President's name. I had known Mr. Ehrlichman for a good ten to twelve years and respected him highly as a man of complete honesty and devotion to duty. . . . Ehrlichman had been named within the White House as the man in charge of stopping security leaks and overhauling the security regulations. The Central Intelligence Agency is charged with safeguarding intelligence sources and methods. From these facts, I then drew the conclusion which I believe any reasonable man would have reached, namely that Howard Hunt had been hired by the White House to act in the security field and that the Central Intelligence Agency was being ordered to assist him.

Hunt drove over to the CIA on July 22, and, according to Cushman's testimony, he "stated that he had a very sensitive one-time interview that the White House wanted him to conduct with a person whose ideology he was not sure of and that he dare not reveal his, Hunt's, true identity." General Cushman said that in his conversation with Hunt he was not able to obtain any details of the interview "which he [Hunt] stated that he had to conduct and he said that on White House orders he was not to reveal the nature and scope of this interview nor the fact that he worked for the White House." Hunt assured him that "he was working to a good purpose in the interests of the country."

Cushman, who had known Hunt for nearly fifteen years, took the precaution of secretly taping this conversation, and the transcript was made public by the Senate Watergate Committee. It makes interesting reading, providing still more insight into Hunt's personality and psychology.

HUNT: Could we make this just the two of us?

CUSHMAN: All right, sure. We certainly can.

HUNT: Thank you very much. I've been charged with quite a highly sensitive mission by the White House to visit and elicit information from an individual whose ideology we aren't entirely sure of, and for that purpose they asked me to come over here and see if you could get me two things: flash alias documentation, which wouldn't have to be back-stopped, and some degree of physical disguise, for a one-time op—in and out.

CUSHMAN: I don't see why we can't. . . .

HUNT: We'll keep it as closely held as possible. I don't know how you or your covert people want to work it, but what I would like would be to meet someone in a "safehouse" . . . We're planning on travelling either Saturday or Sunday. Tomorrow afternoon probably would be the earliest it could be accomplished, so if somebody could do it by tomorrow afternoon, it would be a great job.

For the next few minutes, Hunt and Cushman engaged in light banter about keeping one's weight down. Hunt used this opportunity to impress on Cushman how important he had been before he retired from the CIA the previous year. He said: "Curiously, since I've retired, the thing I've missed most is the gym facilities, because I used to go down there. I'd be there about fifteen minutes before the Director [of the CIA] would arrive, so we'd kind of overlap a bit, and that really kept my weight down, because it discouraged mid-afternoon snacking, you know, and then I didn't feel a need to drink when I got home because I was too tired, you know, so I do miss that facility."

Then the business conversation resumed, and General Cushman asked Hunt whether he could get in touch with him at the White House. Hunt inquired whether his request could be met the following afternoon, and Cushman replied that he would give it "a try," although "I haven't been in this business before, haven't had to."

HUNT: Well, Ehrlichman said that you were the . . .

CUSHMAN: Yes, he called me. I mean, I haven't been in the covert business, so I don't know if they operate real fast, but I suppose they do.

HUNT: Well, I know they can. . . . it's just a question of getting some—some physical disguise.

CUSHMAN: What do you need? That'll be the first thing they'll ask.

HUNT: Well, I'll need, let's see, what have I got here? I probably need just a driver's license and some pocket litter.

CUSHMAN: Driver's license . . .

HUNT: Driver's license in any state at all, I don't care; some pocket litter of some sort—pretty standard stuff.

CUSHMAN: Pocket litter?

HUNT: Yes, that's what they call it.

CUSHMAN: You don't care in what name?

HUNT: I would like the first name to be Edward, that's all, if it could be Edward, because I'm being introduced to this gentleman by just one name. [Edward is of course the English version of "Eduardo," Hunt's cover name during the Bay of Pigs invasion.]

CUSHMAN: And any state for the driver's license?

HUNT: Yes, any state, it doesn't make any difference, and I'm just going to have to check into a hotel, and I'll use this alias documentation for that.

CUSHMAN: Yes.

HUNT: And I'll be talking to the same people in and out, and if it goes a little bit, well, that's swell. . . . You can't be a beggar. . . .

CUSHMAN: OK. Let's see, you gave a number one time where I could get you.

HUNT: Right. Chuck Colson—my office is unappended so far, but—that's a direct line to Colson's office, and my office is two floors up . . . and I'm only there part of the time.

CUSHMAN: All right, fine. Whoever is there can get ahold of you.

HUNT: Anybody can get ahold of me . . .

CUSHMAN: And I can give them—or should I ask for you to call me back?

HUNT: I just—you know, I know so many people out here, it's just as well I'm not seen—if I'm going to put on a physical disguise, it's going to stick. I wouldn't want to be seen walking out of here. I'm sure they've got safe facilities downtown.

CUSHMAN: Yes. They sure as hell did on my last tour of duty here. . . . The place I used to meet people was at an office building—right near where the Press Club is—it was the Washington Building, next door to the Press Club. There used to be a nightclub on the second floor, and we used to meet people up there. I had a gal who thought it was just lots of fun to be in this business. She used to have me meeting people out on the damned park benches and other stuff, and I'd give her hell, if necessary. She just thought it was fun, playing a game. Well, they're keeping you busy with this new . . .

HUNT: Well, they sure are, I'll tell you. But, actually, I'm delighted that they thought about me, and thought to call on me, and that I had the time. This gives me about a twelve-hour day now.

CUSHMAN: Keep you from thinking you retired.

HUNT: I'm not going into retirement . . . I'm convinced that the reason we're doing all this is for a good purpose.

CUSHMAN: Yes.

HUNT: An essential purpose.

CUSHMAN: If you see John Ehrlichman, say "hello" for me.

HUNT: I will, indeed . . . I expect to see him tomorrow.

CUSHMAN: He's an old friend of mine and has got a full platter too.

HUNT: Oh, that he does.

CUSHMAN: How's that Domestic Council working out? You don't hear about it much in this business.

HUNT: It's working out pretty well. Of course, two things that have really electrified the White . . . and I don't know why I'm telling you this because your contacts are undoubtedly much higher than mine over there but, the Pentagon Papers, of course . . .

CUSHMAN: Well, John [Ehrlichman]—I think John is in charge of the security overhaul, isn't he?

HUNT: That's right.

CUSHMAN: Well, I guess that's right. It's sort of a domestic problem rather than a Kissinger problem.

HUNT: That is, indeed . . . I find the same type of compartmentalization over there that I do here.

CUSHMAN: Well, let me get to work on this, and I'll get the word back to you.

HUNT: Yes, and the less my name comes up, absolutely the better.

CUSHMAN: Yes.

HUNT: If you want me to use a pseudonym with this guy—actually, I suppose the best—if he's in the room, I'll get there at the specified time, and I'll just go in and . . .

CUSHMAN: OK, fine, I'll get the word to you on how we'll work it.

What Hunt told General Cushman on July 22 obviously had little to do with plugging news leaks. In fact, he did not even mention news leaks. Looking back at the record, it also appears that Hunt was misleading General Cushman over the reasons for the disguises and false documents. If, indeed, Hunt was planning an interview with a person whose "ideology" was uncertain, both the identity of that person and the purpose of the mission are a mystery to this day. Unless new discoveries are made, one must assume that no such mission was planned.

The next day, the CIA's Technical Services Division dutifully provided Hunt with a red wig (Helms was to insist later that it was "brunette"), a speech-alteration device, a tiny Tessina camera to be hidden in a tobacco pouch (Hunt is a pipe-smoker), tape recorders, and false papers. But existing evidence does not show that Hunt undertook any secret missions whatsoever for at least a month, despite the sense of urgency he had communicated to Cushman.

We do not know whether Hunt was aware, about the same time he was seeing General Cushman, that David Young, the National Security Council official attached to the plumbers, was simultaneously requesting the CIA to prepare a psychological profile of Daniel Ellsberg, apparently with Kissinger's knowledge. Young did this after Dr. Lewis J. Fielding told two FBI agents on July 21 that he would not give them psychiatric data on Ellsberg. The agents had been sent to see him because by now the White House was nearly obsessed with the Ellsberg case. The CIA as a matter of course produces psychological profiles of many foreign leaders and other interesting persons abroad. But, according to Helms's testimony, it had never been done at home with an American citizen as the target. CIA's psychologists and psychiatrists reluctantly undertook to do it as a high-priority task for the White House, but when it was produced in the third week of August, the White House found it unsatisfactory. Young told Ehrlichman in a memorandum, "We have received the CIA preliminary psychological study which, I must say, I am disappointed in and consider very superficial." The reason was that the CIA study found, to the White House's utter amazement, that Ellsberg had been motivated by "what he deemed a higher order of patriotism" in making the Pentagon Papers available to the press two months earlier. Prepared by Dr. Bernard Malloy, a CIA psychologist, the document said that Ellsberg was a brilliant and highly motivated man who considered himself "as having a special mission, and, indeed, as bearing a special responsibility" concerning the Vietnam war. Dr. Malloy reported, "There's no suggestion that the subject [Ellsberg] thought anything treasonous in his act . . . rather, he seemed to be responding to what he deemed a higher order of patriotism. His exclusion of the three volumes of the papers concerned with the secret negotiations [with the North Vietnamese during the Johnson era] would support this. . . . As the data base is fragmentary, and there has been no direct clinical evaluation of the subject, this indirect assessment should be considered highly speculative."

Even with this disclaimer, the CIA study certainly was not what the White House wanted to see. As Ellsberg's trial approached, the White House was keen on creating a devastating image of the man. Under the circumstances, Young requested and received authority from Ehrlichman to undertake "a covert operation . . . to examine all the medical files still held by Ellsberg's psychoanalyst covering the two-year period in which he was undergoing analysis." This covert operation was to be Hunt's first assignment for the White House.

But first, Hunt flew to Miami to talk with "Macho" Barker, his Bay of Pigs companion. Hunt and Barker had not seen each other for almost ten years. They met on April 16, 1971, at a Miami reunion marking the tenth anniversary of the Cuban invasion, when Hunt had not yet joined the Special Unit, and their encounter was purely social. When "Eduardo" returned to Miami in August, however, it was all "White House business" as his friend later told the story. Barker, a stout, bespectacled man who was making a comfortable living in the real-estate business, was quickly convinced by the smooth-talking Hunt that it was his patriotic duty to become a "soldier" in the plumbers unit. Hunt told Barker that the missions were top-secret, involving matters of national security and under the personal authority of the President of the United States. He hinted that it was the question of a traitor who passed vital information to a foreign embassy. Although he did not acquaint Barker with the full plan, Hunt made it clear to him that the success of the planned missions would, in the end, be of benefit to the "liberation" of Cuba from Castro.

Barker, a man of intense loyalties, agreed and promised his old pal "Eduardo" to recruit additional Cuban-American volunteers. Miami was full of brigade veterans and other Cubans who were patriotic, adventurous, and gullible.

Back in Washington, Hunt proceeded to press the CIA for further support. This included the suggestion that a woman stenographer employed in the Paris station of the CIA be assigned to him in the Special Unit. The woman, a friend of Hunt's, was never publicly identified, but it seemed as if Hunt was again acting out one of his novels with Parisian and Washingtonian settings.

Hunt's other requests to the CIA were for car-rental credit cards in his assumed name of Edward J. Hamilton (sometimes he used a set of documents in which his name appeared as Edward Warren) and a New York phone number with an answering service. This led General Cushman to write Helms a memo on August 31, telling him that he had called Ehrlichman to explain why the CIA would no longer meet Hunt's requests and that he was "becoming a pain in the neck." Cushman noted that Ehrlichman promised him that he would "restrain" Hunt. Helms read Cushman's memo and wrote "Good!" on it.

Even though the CIA seemed to be slamming the door on Hunt, he already had the equipment necessary for the Ellsberg burglary, and he had his orders from Young and Krogh to go after Ellsberg's files. To the Senate Committee in 1973, John Dean testified that Krogh had said the instructions for the raid came "directly from the Oval Office." Liddy told Hunt some time in August that the FBI was no longer in shape to undertake the Ellsberg "bag-job" and that the White House lacked sufficient confidence in the Secret Service. This was as close as anyone connected with the White House—if one is to believe Hunt—ever came to admitting that the Presidency was determined to run its own intelligence operations. Hunt himself told a Congressional committee in 1973 that he was advised by his superiors that nobody directly associated with the White House could conduct an operation of this type. This was a rather semantic distinction, because Hunt, after all, was on the White House payroll as a consultant—secret as his employment was being kept. In any event, he was asked to try his old CIA contacts in Miami, and this led to the recruiting visit to Barker.

On August 25, Hunt and Liddy flew to Los Angeles to "case" the building where Dr. Fielding's office was located. They entered Dr. Fielding's office—he was away—under some excuse and took pictures. But they did not touch the files. Outside, Hunt photographed a smiling Liddy standing in front of the wall with the plaque bearing the psychiatrist's name in the background. Hunt then telephoned a contact at the CIA in Langley asking to be met the following morning at Dulles International Airport. The pair were met by two CIA agents from the Technical Services Division to whom they handed film to be developed from Hunt's tiny camera.

The CIA developed the photographs, but that same afternoon, August 26, orders came from the top that Hunt should no longer be aided by the Agency. As Cushman testified, he and Helms decided to drop Hunt because he "was becoming more and more unreasonable and demanding, and was attempting to go far beyond the scope of the original instructions which I had given, and which related to his statement that he had a one-time interview operation to conduct." It was evidently dawning on CIA's officials that the Agency was being used for unclear purposes which, in time, might become embarrassing. This was sound foresight. In fact, Cushman went further and advised Ehrlichman on August 27 that the assistance being requested from the CIA by Hunt could be construed as improper under the law. Cushman testified that he also advised Ehrlichman that, "in my opinion, Mr. Hunt was of questionable judgment. He should know better than to ask for such support. Therefore, I made this recommendation to Mr. Ehrlichman for him to do with as he deemed proper." Ehrlichman evidently was unconcerned with Cushman's opinions about Hunt's judgment, because nothing was done to halt the second part of the Ellsberg mission.

During the Labor Day weekend, Hunt, Liddy, Barker, and two Cubans he employed as real-estate salesmen flew to Los Angeles. The latter were Eugenio R. Martinez and Felipe De-Diego. Both were Bay of Pigs veterans and had had subsequent experience in CIA's clandestine operations against Cuba. Martinez, in fact, was still on a $100-a-month CIA retainer, which he kept until after the Watergate break-in almost a year later. (Helms testified that only after the 1972 adventure did the Agency realize that Martinez was on its payroll.) On the evening of September 3, Barker, Martinez, and DeDiego broke a window on the ground floor and forced the door into Dr. Fielding's office. Earlier, Martinez and DeDiego had gone there wearing the uniforms of a local delivery service and had left a green suitcase addressed to the psychiatrist. Now, they opened the suitcase and took out a camera, film, and lights. Barker broke into two file cabinets while Martinez and DeDiego photographed several files. Hunt was stationed near Dr. Fielding's home to be certain that the psychiatrist did not suddenly decide to go to his office. Liddy was driving a rented car around the office building to be able to warn the raiders in case a police cruiser appeared in the vicinity. All of them were in communication by walkie-talkie. The burglary was a success, except that there were no Ellsberg files in the office and the Cubans had photographed other ones. So the operation turned out to be a fiasco, something that occurred with disturbing frequency in operations mounted by Howard Hunt.

After they had returned to Washington, Hunt and Liddy told their associates that they had failed to produce the files the White House wanted so badly. Young and Krogh proposed that the unit repeat the break-in at Dr. Fielding's home—they thought he might have kept the Ellsberg data there—but Ehrlichman apparently vetoed this. In fact, he testified that he told the unit not to engage any more in such enterprises. It is an interesting point, however, that Ehrlichman never told Nixon about the Beverly Hills raid. The President, according to his statement in August 1973, only learned about it in the spring of 1973. So much for good judgment in the Nixon White House.

Hunt felt no remorse about the Ellsberg operation. In 1973, he told the federal grand jury in Washington that it had been simply a clandestine action under the auspices of "proper authority." Ehrlichman also defended this mission as one in the national interest and therefore justifiable. As one read transcripts of the testimony and listened to the Senate Committee hearings, one had the chilling sensation that the White House men, from Ehrlichman all the way down to Hunt, lived in a private world and spoke a different ethical language from the rest of us.

Defending the Ellsberg raid, Ehrlichman told the Senators that he assumed that

[Hunt and Liddy] had a complete defense, in the sense that they were operating according to what they believed to be authorization. The reaction that I had to this when I heard about it was one of surprise and disapproval. . . . At that point in time, there were two what I suppose you would arguably call conflicting duties. To have imposed some kind of discipline, to have them arrested, something of this kind, has been suggested as one of the alternatives. Obviously, the other alternative was to pursue this national-security investigation as vigorously as we could and not compromise it, if we could possibly avoid it. You get into these conflicting duty situations, as you know, at times, and you have to take the main chance. You have to do the thing that is more important to the country, and not do the other thing.

The rest of the White House staff, which also kept Nixon in the dark, never told the CIA about the burglary in Beverly Hills. Instead, they requested another psychological profile on Ellsberg. The Agency reluctantly agreed, under heavy pressure from Pennsylvania Avenue. But the second study, produced in November, was no more satisfactory to the White House than the first one. As Helms testified, David Young had "pled" [sic] with him for help, saying that Ellsberg's profile was necessary to stop leaks of classified government information. The extraordinary thing was that nobody seemed to question the essential incongruity of such a request, though Cushman had sent Helms a memorandum warning him that Hunt's activities were drawing the CIA "into a sensitive area of domestic operations against Americans."

The raid on Dr. Fielding's office became public knowledge only in May 1973, while Daniel Ellsberg was on trial. President Nixon said that he learned about it on March 17 from the Justice Department. Helms and Cushman, who no longer are with the CIA, heard about it from newspapers and television. But several other matters remain unexplained in the CIA's attitude toward Hunt. In the first place, it appears that the Agency did not actually halt all its assistance to Hunt, despite the top-level decision at the end of August 1971 to do so. According to Representative Lucien N. Nedzi, Chairman of the House Armed Services Sub-Committee on Intelligence Operations, the Helms-Cushman decision to cut off Hunt "was not disseminated throughout the Agency." Hunt returned to the CIA headquarters in Langley in September to examine certain Agency files, which requires special permission, and in October, a packet of documents concerning a 1954 security leak was delivered to Hunt at his White House office by a CIA courier.

In the second place, there is no satisfactory explanation as to why the CIA never bothered to investigate Hunt's activities even after the Watergate break-in and his identification with it. This was the time when the White House was trying to implicate the CIA in the raid. But Helms told the Senate Committee that he had no idea to what uses, other than the Ellsberg raid (about which he learned almost a year later), Hunt might have put the equipment given him by the CIA. Besides, he told the Senators, it was the FBI's business to investigate all the ramifications of

Watergate and its background, although the CIA did check its records right after the burglary to discover that Eugenio Martinez, one of the Ellsberg burglars also present at Watergate, was still on an Agency retainer.

As this is written, we know of only three operations carried out by Hunt during 1971. One was the Ellsberg operation in late August and early September. The second related to a Kennedy matter. Earlier, Hunt had gone to Rhode Island to persuade a government employee who once had contacts with the Kennedy family to provide him with "dirt" on Senator Edward M. Kennedy and the Chappaquiddick incident. He also spent long hours in the White House library reading up on Chappaquiddick. (Ulasewicz had started investigating the same matter for the White House in 1969.) It seems rather doubtful that Hunt was referring to his trip to Rhode Island when he told Cushman that he needed the disguises and false documentation to meet a person whose ideology he doubted. Hunt the novelist was a master at doing and saying improbable things. But at that time he happened to be finishing a novel, *The Coven*, whose main and repulsive personage, Senator Newbold Vane, is obviously a Kennedy composite image.

Hunt's third effort during 1971 was the forgery of top-secret State Department telegrams in order to prove that President Kennedy had personally and specifically ordered the assassination of the deposed South Vietnamese President, Ngo Dinh Diem, and his brother, Ngo Dinh Nhu. This particular bit of malfeasance was done in September, shortly after the Beverly Hills burglary, apparently on Colson's orders. It was a classical "disinformation" action of the kind that the CIA and KGB have been practicing over the years. It was certainly a strange way of preventing national-security leaks to the press, although the White House was to insist after Watergate that plugging leaks had been the purpose of the plumbers unit. What happened, of course, was that the ever-imaginative Colson had conceived this operation in order to embarrass the Democrats during the approaching Presidential campaign. Hunt first tried to obtain top-secret "backchannel" telegrams from the Pentagon and the CIA, but he was turned down cold. David Young, who had close contacts in the State Department because of his earlier work on Kissinger's staff, telephoned William Macomber, then a Deputy Under Secretary of State, to obtain the Department's secret telegrams on Vietnam for Hunt. Macomber obliged. With Colson more or less looking over his shoulder, Hunt worked with a pair of scissors and a Xerox machine to forge incriminating telegrams. The next step was to summon a *Life* magazine reporter and show him the product of Hunt's work, in the hopes that *Life* would fall for this deception. The reporter, however, had the good sense to file away his notes about the phony telegrams and forget about them.

Whatever else Hunt may have done during that year (Nixon, as I have said, hinted in August 1973 that the Special Unit had other national-security assignments that must be kept secret), White House records show that he charged for sixty-three days of consultant work, adding up to a total of $8190. Besides, the White House bankrolled his expense account, which must have been considerable, inasmuch as Howard the *bon vivant* was inclined to stay at the best hotels and eat at the best restaurants. Hunt also allowed vanity to prevail over security, which seemed so important in the work of the Special Unit, and rewrote his listing for the 1972–73 edition of *Who's Who,* describing himself as a "public relations executive" and giving the White House as his only office address.

One of the crucial, unanswered questions about Hunt's activities for the White House was whether he was ever promised executive clemency for himself and his associates in the event they were caught in one of their operations. This issue is central because it touches upon the absolutely vital point of whether President Nixon was aware beforehand of all these "dirty tricks" and had, in effect, authorized them. In the context of the entire question of Presidential credibility, Hunt becomes immensely important. But the President reaffirmed in his August 15, 1973, statement that he never authorized clemency for the Watergate defendants. He told Ehrlichman in July 1972, a few weeks after the burglary, that "under no circumstances would executive clemency be considered" in this affair. Hunt also testified that he was never promised clemency. Bitterly, he told the Senators that the White House had tried to disown him.

Another mystery is whether Hunt, possibly acting on his own, assured Barker and his Cuban-American team that clemency would be forthcoming after a year or so in prison, should anyone be caught, and that during any time in prison their "salaries" would be paid and their families looked after. Hatred of Fidel Castro or not, it is a fair question whether the Miami men would have risked so much without this kind of assurance. And it is a fact that between July 1972 and mid-1973 more than $450,000 were paid to the Watergate defendants and their families and lawyers. Most of the money came from a White House cash fund.

What is known from John Dean's testimony is that, using John Caulfield and Anthony Ulasewicz (the two White House investigators), Dean allegedly sent a message to McCord, one of the jailed Watergate raiders, telling him that executive clemency would be granted if he remained silent about any "higher-ups" involved in the scheme. Dean's emissaries reportedly told McCord that this word was coming from "the very highest levels of the White House." Dean's testimony before the Senate Committee showed that prior to the sentencing of the Watergate conspirators in March 1973, Ehrlichman and Dean inquired from Richard G. Kleindienst, then Attorney General, how soon clemency could be granted to the convicted men. Dean claimed that he could be encouraging to McCord once John Mitchell, the onetime Attorney General and later head of the Committee to Re-Elect the President, advised him that a Presidential pardon could be expected. Dean testified that Mitchell indicated to him that promises of clemency had likewise been given Howard Hunt. Moreover, Dean told the Senate panel, Ehrlichman, having checked it out with Nixon, had informed Colson that clemency could be promised to Hunt. Dean also said that the President told *him* on March 13, 1973, that he had discussed clemency with Ehrlichman and Colson. Subsequently, the President, Ehrlichman, Colson, and Mitchell flatly denied that clemency was ever contemplated or offered to Hunt and his associates. My own impression is that at least the Cuban-Americans were led by someone to believe that they would be granted clemency. Only two weeks after the Watergate burglary, a lawyer for the Miami group told me that he was certain that for reasons of high loyalty all the raiders would remain silent forever. The Cuban-Americans would plead guilty to avoid testifying at their trial, he said, and they were ready to go to prison, because they knew that their actual time behind bars would be short.

Finally, there remains the related and also unanswered question whether Nixon authorized, before or after the Watergate burglary, hush money for the Watergate defendants, their families, and their lawyers. Dean said that Nixon asked him how much such blackmail would cost, and that he had replied it would be around $1 million, to which Nixon replied that the money should be no problem. This was early in 1973, after the Watergate trial, when Hunt took the initiative of asking the White House for very large sums of money in return for silence on his part and that of his associates. H. R. Haldeman contradicted Dean's interpretation of Nixon's comments about hush money, saying that the President had told Dean "it would be wrong" to pay blackmail money. As for Nixon himself, he claimed in August 1973 that he had been told by his staff only five months earlier that money was being given the defendants, and it was only for the families and attorneys. He added that "one of the defendants," obviously Hunt, was asking $120,000 in return for silence about activities other than the Watergate burglary. The record shows, of course, that nearly half a million dollars was secretly given to the defendants, their families, and lawyers after the Watergate arrests. Now why was such an enormous amount of money paid out, if the White House had no need, as Nixon stated himself, to hide the possible involvement of the nation's top officials in the whole affair? Haldeman told the Senate that these payments were "humanitarian," but half a million dollars does sound a bit high for this. There also is abundant testimony that before her death, Dorothy Hunt was the most active agent in transmitting money requests from her husband to Colson and other White House officials. Even when a Watergate Defendants Relief Fund was set up in Miami to help the men and their families, it turned out that most of the money for it came secretly in cash from Washington, so that the impression could be maintained that the Cuban community was solidly behind the raiders. But this was never the case.

As December 1971 turned into January 1972, Hunt stepped up his activities. He shuttled between his office at the Mullen company and the "Room 16" headquarters in the White House complex one block away. Occasionally, he conferred with Liddy at his office in the Mullen firm. He traveled extensively to Florida and California to organize his task force and to plan his next coup. He drove around Washington in a new Chevrolet with a red, white and blue "Re-elect the President" bumper sticker. The other Hunt family car, a Pontiac, had an American flag decal on one window. He was in his element; he was happy and fulfilled as he had not been in many years; he was close to the power center of the United States government. He exercised power in his own right, applying to the American domestic scene foreign intelligence tactics he had used for twenty-three years with the CIA. The year between July 1971, when he became a "plumber," and June 1972, when the Watergate fiasco occurred, was probably the happiest in Howard Hunt's life. "You see, our government trains people like myself to do these things, and do them successfully. It becomes a way of life for a person like me."

At the White House, it was again this "way of life" for Hunt. The pace of his activities quickened with the new year. He made a number of trips to Miami to discuss future missions with Barker. On one or two occasions, Barker came to Washington to meet Hunt, who kept emphasizing that the success of the operations—as well as President Nixon's re-election—would help Cuba. Barker recalls that Hunt told him at one point that his "national security" organization was "above both the CIA and the FBI." Barker's own reaction to Hunt's entreaties was clearcut: "Mr. Hunt's position in the White House would be a decisive factor at a later date for obtaining help in the liberation of Cuba." At one of the Miami meetings, Hunt told Barker, "Get your men in training going up and down the stairs. They must be in good physical shape." Barker had already recruited Martinez and De-Diego for Hunt, and now he combed the Miami Cuban community for more recruits.

At that stage, there were two separate *agitprop* operations working out of the White House. There was Hunt and Liddy working out of Room 16 and the Miami Cubans being groomed for future missions. The other operation, controlled by H. R. Haldeman, the White House Chief of Staff, was chiefly concerned with a whole range of activities against the Democratic party and its candidates. This included spying on Democratic officials and candidates, trying to sabotage Democratic rallies, and planting informers and provocateurs in Democratic ranks. The principal operator here was the young California lawyer Donald Segretti, who was being paid by President Nixon's personal lawyer, Herbert W. Kalmbach. But early in 1972, it occurred to Haldeman and Colson that it would be a good idea to merge the two operations. One reason was that the White House wanted to run an intensive anti-Democratic campaign in Florida. It had an eye not only on the approaching Democratic primaries in that state but also on the Democratic Convention, which was to be held in Miami Beach. The White House was planning on arranging maximum disturbances—pure "disinformation" right out of *agitprop* textbooks. Since it was Senator Muskie whom Nixon feared the most, the surreptitious "pro-McGovern" strategy in the primaries was to concentrate, through all available means, on infiltrating the Muskie campaign and defaming him in every possible way. The Republicans did little to attack McGovern during that early, preconvention period.

The merger of the two White House groups coincided with Liddy's transfer from the White House to a new post as general counsel to the Committee to Re-Elect the President. The basic idea was that all the intelligence and "dirty tricks" operations should henceforth be centered at the Committee CREEP headquarters. Although Hunt was still theoretically a White House consultant, he was now working hand-in-hand with Liddy. The two of them presently took over the supervision of Segretti's operations. Early in February 1972, Hunt and Liddy flew to Miami with Segretti to firm up the details in the running of the merged intelligence-and-mischief schemes.

But before dedicating himself full time to these disruptive election-year activities, Hunt performed a special job for his White House friend, Chuck Colson. This was a secret trip in mid-March to Denver in order to convince Dita Beard, a Washington lobbyist for the International Telephone and Telegraph Corporation, that she should announce that her memorandum about ITT, the administration, and the relations between them was actually a fraud. ITT had already been a problem for the Nixon administration for some time, as something of a scandal was developing over the Justice Department's favorable settlement of antitrust actions against the huge corporation. Jack Anderson had published what he described as an internal memorandum written by Mrs. Beard stating that the Justice Department had settled the suit against ITT after ITT promised to provide $400,000 to the Republican party for their convention, which was to have been held in San Diego. Early in March, Mrs. Beard was secretly flown from Washington to Denver (apparently by Gordon Liddy), where she interned herself in a local hospital allegedly because of a heart condition.

Colson has admitted that a few days later, he sent Hunt to Denver to "interview" Mrs. Beard concerning the authenticity of the compromising document. Colson ordered Hunt's expedition after Bob Bennett, the friendly president of the Mullen public-relations firm, told him that a private investigating agency working for ITT had concluded that the Beard memo might be a forgery. This private investigating firm was Intertel, also employed on a retainer basis by the Howard Hughes interests. And, of course, Bennett was Hughes's local representative.

For his interview with Mrs. Beard, Hunt wore the CIA's red wig and used the name Edward J. Hamilton. This was the name that appeared on his identification papers prepared by the CIA the previous summer. Much later, when Hunt became identified with Watergate, Mrs. Beard's son Robert told about the visit. "From pictures I've seen, the visitor could have been Howard Hunt. But I couldn't tell. The man refused to identify himself. He seemed to have inside information about what would happen next. . . ." He described the man as "very eerie, he did have a huge red wig on cock-eyed, like he put it on in a dark car. I couldn't have identified my brother if he was dressed like that." We do not know what Hunt said to Mrs. Beard, but she did issue a public statement a few days later saying that, "I did not prepare it [the memo] and could not have. . . . I have done nothing to be ashamed of, and my family and I—and in a greater sense, the whole American government—are the victims of a cruel fraud." Jack Anderson subsequently testified before a Senate committee that Mrs. Beard had confirmed the authenticity of the memo, "line-by-line," with him in an interview on February 24, before going to Denver.

Hunt's employment as a White House consultant terminated officially on March 29 (the records show that in 1972 he had worked in his consulting capacity for twenty-four days, receiving $2120), but, evidently, this had no effect on his continuing operations. In fact, he retained his White House top-secret clearance, as well as a desk and a safe in the White House office where the "plumbers" had previously worked. The contents of this safe were later to become a major issue. It was naturally Colson who arranged for Hunt's formal transfer to the Committee to Re-Elect the President. Jeb Stuart Magruder, a Haldeman and Colson protégé, who was in effective charge of the Committee, testified that he received a telephone call from one of Colson's assistants who "indicated that Mr. Hunt had completed his assignments at the White House, and since we were now involved in intelligence activities, he thought I would find Mr. Hunt was very valuable. . . . I had only met Mr. Hunt once, so I was not really quite sure in what terms he would be valuable. So I indicated . . . that he should return Mr. Hunt to Mr. Liddy."

A few weeks earlier, on March 7, a mysterious tragedy affected the Hunts. Dr. Gary D. Morris, a suburban Washington psychiatrist whose patients included Dorothy Hunt, vanished with his wife during a motorboat outing off Saint Lucia in the Caribbean. The disappearance was never explained and subsequently they were declared legally dead. Friends said that Dorothy was deeply upset over this incident. (In 1973, federal investigators began looking into the Morris story.)

Liddy, who had done the Ellsberg "bag-job" with Hunt the

previous September, was delighted to have Hunt aboard. He put him in charge of Segretti's operation and of recruiting Republican agents to infiltrate Democratic campaigns. Presently, Hunt found at least one volunteer in Washington and proceeded to run a miniature CIA-type clandestine operation. His infiltrator was Tom Gregory, a student from Brigham Young University in Utah, who on Hunt's instructions offered his services to Muskie headquarters in Washington. Gregory was attached to the Muskie campaign's foreign-policy section. Throughout March, he supplied Hunt with information on Muskie's traveling and speaking plans, the structure of his organization, and even the quarrels within the group. In the best conspiratorial fashion, Hunt and Gregory met every Friday at a drugstore in downtown Washington. Gregory would hand over an envelope with several typewritten sheets representing his weekly report. In return, Hunt slipped him an envelope containing $175, which was Gregory's weekly salary. It was just like being in the CIA all over again. Liddy and Hunt also arranged to rent space next door to the Muskie offices to be used for monitoring telephone conversations. But the bugging, for some reason, was never initiated.

While Hunt busied himself with his missions, the Re-Election Committee at 1701 Pennsylvania Avenue approved on March 30 a plan devised by Liddy to arrange for surreptitious entry into the Washington offices of the Democratic National Committee in order to plant telephone bugs and to photograph documents in the files. After long discussions, $250,000 was approved at a final conference on Key Biscayne, off Miami, for this operation, which received the code name of Project Gemstone. Liddy's scheme also provided for the same type of secret surveillance at the Fontainebleau Hotel in Miami, where most of the Democratic leaders would be staying during the convention in June, and the headquarters of the party's nominee after his selection. That was when the idea of the Watergate break-in was actually born.

In April, Hunt performed a signal service for the Committee to

Re-Elect the President. A new law on campaign contributions had set April 7, 1972, as the deadline for confidential donations. From that date on, the names of all campaign contributors and the amounts donated by them had to be publicly disclosed, along with an accounting of the expenditures. Inasmuch as the White House and the Committee to Re-Elect were deeply involved in an aggressive fund-raising campaign—it included virtual extortion from heads of big corporations—a tremendous rush developed to collect as much money as possible before April 7. Between March 10 and April 7, the Republicans managed to collect more than $15 million in contributions they expected to remain anonymous and unaccounted. But when it developed that all the money could not be remitted in time, the Committee hit upon the idea of "laundering" the money abroad. Thus, checks totaling $89,000 were sent after April 7 by the Committee's Texas Finance Chairman to a Mexico City lawyer who represented his interests there. The lawyer deposited the checks in a Mexican bank which, in turn, issued a number of checks totaling $89,000. These were forwarded to Bernard Barker, Hunt's right-hand man, in Miami. Barker deposited them in his Miami bank. A few days later, he withdrew most of the money in cash; it was then sent to Washington and placed in a safe in the office of Maurice H. Stans, former Secretary of Commerce and chief financial officer of the Committee to Re-Elect. In one way or another, Hunt and his cohorts seemed to be involved in almost every aspect of secret Republican operations. When George Wallace was shot near Washington, Colson quickly dispatched Hunt to Milwaukee to "get a line" on Arthur Bremer, the assailant.

Hunt was simultaneously activating his Cuban team for a whole series of weird missions. J. Edgar Hoover, the FBI Director, died on the morning of May 2. Hunt found out that there were plans for Hoover's body to lie in state at the Capitol the following day. He immediately contacted Barker in Miami and ordered him to come up to Washington as soon as possible with his "boys" to disrupt anticipated antiwar demonstrations which some time before Hoover's death had been scheduled for May 3 and 4 on the west steps of the Capitol.

Barker instantly organized his squad. It included Frank Sturgis, a friend of Hunt's, and Reinaldo Pico, a Cuban exile who had fought in the invading brigade at the Bay of Pigs. As Pico recalled it later in a newspaper interview, Barker told him "there are hippies and men who are traitors to this country and democracy, who are going to make demonstrations and perpetrate an outrage to Hoover." Barker and seven other men flew to Washington the same evening and awaited instructions from Hunt in a downtown hotel. On the afternoon of May 3, the Barker team went to the Capitol, where Daniel Ellsberg was one of the antiwar speakers. Barker knocked down a long-haired young man, and Sturgis hit another demonstrator. The police arrested Barker and Sturgis, but they were immediately released with a warning, after a man in a gray suit told the lieutenant in charge that they were "anticommunists and good men." This was the sum total of the results produced by Hunt's first Washington operation. The Cubans went home to Miami the following morning.

Concurrently with these operations, Hunt's people began combing Miami for rooms for demonstrators that the Nixon people hoped to bring from out of town to disrupt the Democratic Presidential Convention.

For reasons that still remain mysterious, Hunt had procured for himself on January 7, 1972, a Mexican tourism card, valid for three months, in the name of Edward J. Hamilton, the name that appeared on his CIA-fashioned papers. On the card Hunt represented himself as a New Jersey–born lawyer residing in Massachusetts. (The CIA had given Hunt a Massachusetts driver's license.) Later, reports circulated that Hunt had a task force in Mexico for a "national security" job in Panama.

A strange incident took place at the Chilean Embassy in Washington on the night of May 13, a weekend. Unidentified persons broke into the embassy chancellery and rifled the files of Orlando Letelier, Chile's Ambassador to the United States, and of the embassy's First Secretary. Subsequently it turned out that the burglars took some documents. The embassy summoned the police, but it developed that the raiders left no fingerprints. They must have used gloves. The Chilean diplomats, who also informed the State Department, obviously wondered about the burglary, but only after the Watergate raid did they become suspicious that the embassy might have been a victim of Hunt's operatives. Hunt may have theorized that incriminating documents of some kind could be found at the embassy, linking Allende's government with the Democratic party. It must be remembered that for a long time the administration was obsessed with the thought that many radical activities in America were being financed from abroad, especially from Cuba. This was never proved, of course, and, in fact, the FBI reported later that there were no grounds for such allegations. After the Watergate raid, John Dean told the new Deputy Director of the CIA, General Vernon A. Walters, that members of the Hunt-Barker group might have done the Chilean Embassy job. (And Jack Anderson wrote that Frank Sturgis, whom he knew, and Eugenio Martinez, who had helped to raid Dr. Fielding's office, might have been involved.)

The pattern continued. At dawn on May 16, someone broke into the offices of a law firm in the Watergate, where the Democratic National Committee also had its headquarters. This, too, was suspicious because among the partners in the firm were Sargent Shriver, John Kennedy's brother-in-law (and subsequently McGovern's running mate); Patricia Roberts Harris, chairman of the Credentials Committee for the Democratic Convention; and Max M. Kampelman, an adviser to Hubert Humphrey. Kampelman was long regarded as an "enemy" of the White House.

Somewhere along the line, Colson and Hunt reportedly discussed the idea of fire-bombing the offices of the Brookings Institution in Washington. Brookings is a think-tank whose members study both foreign and domestic issues. Its staff includes a number of former senior officials of the Kennedy and Johnson administrations as well as several ex-staffers of Kissinger's National Security Council. The fire-bombing never took place and, subsequently, Colson said the whole discussion was in the nature of a joke.

Howard Hunt's next operation, however, was no joke. On May 22, Barker arrived in Washington with a five-man team from Miami. Each man carried false papers. Barker came as "Frank Carter," Martinez as "Jene Valdez," Sturgis as "Joseph D'Alberto," Pico as "Joe Granada," DeDiego (another veteran of Beverly Hills) as "Jose Piedra," and the team's lock-picker, Virgilio Ramon Gonzalez, as "Raul Godoy." Pico said later that Barker had told him that "there were persons who were going to protest in front of the White House or other places and asked me if I was willing to go. . . . I said I was. I always considered that 'Macho' was inspired by true patriotic fervor." So, the men appear to have been brought to Washington under false pretenses. This, as we have seen, was nothing new.

All the indications are that Hunt brought the team from Miami to prepare the Watergate break-in in detail. On the evening of May 23, Hunt presided over a planning session in Barker's hotel bedroom. The whole Miami team was present, and Hunt brought along Liddy, McCord (the security chief for the Committee to Re-Elect the President and the electronics expert for Project Gemstone), and Tom Gregory, the student informer. Nothing was said about actions against antiwar demonstrators; instead, Hunt and Liddy told the group that they would be involved in a double mission of breaking into the headquarters of the Democratic National Committee and the McGovern headquarters. Detailed instructions were given, and McCord demonstrated his electronic equipment, including walkie-talkies, for the benefit of the Miami team.

For the next three days, the Miami men had nothing to do. But in the afternoon of May 26, they moved to the Watergate Hotel, which adjoins the Watergate office building on Virginia Avenue, and checked in under their false names. Hunt checked in separately as "Edward Warren" (his other cover name) and Liddy as "George Leonard." There was still another man in the picture. He was Alfred C. Baldwin III, a former FBI agent, Marine Corps captain, and graduate student from Southern Connecticut State College.

Baldwin had been hired on May 1 by McCord for the security staff of the Committee to Re-Elect, with the specific assignment of acting as a security guard for Martha Mitchell, wife of the former Attorney General (who was still the Committee's head). After less than two weeks of guarding Mrs. Mitchell, McCord reassigned Baldwin to carry out secret surveillance of radicals in Washington. McCord installed him in a room at the Howard Johnson Motor Lodge, directly across the street from the Watergate building. Baldwin was spending a few days in Connecticut when Hunt assembled his raiders in Washington. Returning to his room at the Motor Lodge, Baldwin saw with astonishment that McCord had installed a sophisticated radio receiver, walkie-talkies, tapes, and other electronic equipment there. Baldwin said later that McCord told him, "We're going to put some units over there tonight (pointing to the Watergate office building), and you'll be monitoring them." During that same afternoon, Hunt and Liddy came to Baldwin's room to look over the monitoring equipment. In the early evening, a final planning session was held in Hunt's room in the Watergate Hotel. Then Baldwin and McCord went back to the Motor Lodge while Hunt, Liddy, and the Miami raiders went to dinner in the Continental Room, a private conference room in the Watergate office building. A believer in largesse, Hunt arranged for the Watergate Hotel to serve the dinner, which cost $236.

At midnight, the raiders went to work. Hunt and Gonzalez, the locksmith, posted themselves in a corridor adjoining the Continental Room. Liddy and the rest of the Cuban-American team went across the street to the Motor Lodge. Hunt's idea was that Gonzalez would jimmy the lock on a door connecting the corridor with the first-floor landing; from there, Hunt and Gonzalez would go up the stairwell and to the sixth-floor offices of the Democratic National Committee. But Gonzalez could not open the door. The waiters who had served the dinner had then locked the Continental Room area, with the result that Hunt and Gonzalez were trapped until dawn, when finally they managed to get out. Once more, a Hunt operation had turned into a farce. Hunt told Liddy over the walkie-talkie that he was making no progress, so Liddy took charge of the second mission, the proposed raid on the McGovern headquarters near the Capitol. Liddy took three Cubans with him, while McCord and Baldwin followed in another car. Liddy, a gun fancier, carried an attaché case containing a high-powered pellet pistol. But because a drunk had parked himself for the night in front of the McGovern headquarters, the group decided to give the raid up and they went home to bed at dawn.

The following night, May 27, Hunt himself did the preparatory work, but that, too, failed, as the team could not get inside. On May 28, the third attempt was made. Hunt himself taped the latch on the door leading from the garage (which serves both the Watergate Hotel and the office building) to the stairwell, and the doors from the stairwell to the sixth and seventh floors. (This was a CIA technique that Hunt had described in one of his novels.) Presently, Hunt returned to his hotel room. Now it was the turn of the Barker team to go into the Democratic party headquarters, taking advantage of the taped doors. The raiders wore rubber gloves and carried special cameras and flashlights. Once inside the office, Barker radioed Hunt that his squad was safely inside. Shortly before 2 A.M., McCord joined them in the Democratic offices and proceeded to install telephone taps on several instruments in the suite occupied by Lawrence O'Brien, Democratic National Chairman. Simultaneously, Barker busied himself looking "for documents indicating contributions from Cuba or from leftist organizations, and those inclined to violence." Although no such documents seemed to exist, Barker found a number of other papers, including one detailing security arrangements for the Democratic National Convention, which he had Martinez photograph under a light held by two other Cubans. Another document was a copy of a routine letter signed by O'Brien. Just before 4 A.M., the raid was completed. On the same night, a half-hearted effort had been made to case the McGovern headquarters—this also on Hunt's instructions—but it failed and was never attempted again.

For the next two weeks, Baldwin, sitting in his room at the Motor Lodge, monitored telephone conversations at the Democratic headquarters. (The monitoring operation was limited because one of the bugs did not work.) Only a few of the conversations had to do with politics. The Democrats seemed to chat mainly about personal matters. Baldwin turned over typed transcripts of these conversations to McCord, who in turn had Liddy's secretary retype them on "Gemstone" stationery. The transcripts carried such codes as "Ruby 1," "Ruby 2," and "Crystal." Liddy gave the final transcript to Magruder, who allegedly showed them to Mitchell. Magruder testified later that the transcripts were virtually useless, and Mitchell denied ever seeing them. Nonetheless, Magruder made them available to an aide to Haldeman, because the White House was the ultimate consumer of this intelligence. When Haldeman testified before the Senate Committee, he said he could not recall seeing any Watergate transcripts.

In any event, it was made clear to Hunt and Liddy that the information they were obtaining from Watergate did not seem to warrant the risks and the expense. So Hunt and Liddy conceived the idea of going back to the Democratic offices to improve their bugging system. This was their undoing.

Howard Hunt and Gordon Liddy picked Friday, June 16, as "D-day" for the second major Watergate mission. Again, Hunt was master-minding the strategy, tactics, and details. Again McCord and Baldwin were the two professional security men. (McCord had returned on June 12 from a six-day visit in Miami, where, he said, he was checking out security arrangements for the Democratic and Republican conventions. Presumably, his interest in the security of the Democrats was of a different nature from his interest in Republican security.)

In the afternoon of June 12, McCord instructed Baldwin to go across the street from the Motor Lodge to the Democratic headquarters to find out precisely where Larry O'Brien's office was located on the sixth floor. Apparently, the first raid had been partially unsuccessful because Hunt's men did not know just exactly where to place all the telephone transmitter bugs. Introducing himself as the nephew of a former Democratic National Committee chairman, Baldwin was shown around the place and made mental notes as to the exact location of O'Brien's private office. The following day, Hunt telephoned Barker in Miami and told him to come up to Washington in the afternoon of June 16, along with the team that was picked for the impending operation.

Barker, accompanied by Sturgis, Martinez, and Gonzalez, arrived at Washington's National Airport in the afternoon and, following Hunt's instructions, drove directly to the Watergate Hotel, where two rooms, each on a different floor, had been reserved for them. Each room cost $38 a night; evidently money was no object in Hunt's operations. Shortly thereafter, Hunt, Liddy, and McCord arrived, and the whole group had a lobster dinner on the Watergate Hotel terrace. It was a pleasant June evening in Washington.

Carrying out the first part of Hunt's plan, McCord walked down the stairwell of the hotel to the garage. McCord quickly put tape on two doors leading to the stairwell in the office building, and then went to the Motor Lodge, where he spent about three hours working with Baldwin on the bugging and monitoring equipment. Hunt, Liddy, Barker, Sturgis, Martinez, and Gonzalez nervously waited in Room 214 in the Watergate Hotel. Shortly after 1 A.M.—it was now June 17—McCord telephoned Hunt from the Motor Lodge to say that the Democratic headquarters appeared to be empty, for the last light in its office had just been turned off. Leaving Baldwin at the monitor console, McCord strolled across the street to join the others in the Watergate hotel room. At precisely that moment, Frank Wills, a twenty-four-year-old security guard, found the tape on the two doors leading from the garage to the office building's stairwell. Not giving the tapes a second thought, Wills removed them and continued on his rounds. In Room 214, Hunt gave the go-ahead to launch the operation.

As usual, Hunt considered himself a staff officer—the mastermind—who safely stays behind and directs operations by remote control while his men, the soldiers, do the actual risky work. This had been true in Beverly Hills at Dr. Fielding's office, and again during the first Watergate break-in. Hunt's explanation for this is that he could not risk arrest because of his White House connections. But McCord was the Republicans' security chief, which was just as bad in the case of capture.

Thus, as McCord, Barker, Sturgis, Martinez, and Gonzalez sneaked down to the garage, Howard Hunt and Gordon Liddy stayed behind in Room 214. Hunt puffed on his pipe, and Liddy blew clouds of cigar smoke. To assure swift communications, Hunt had a walkie-talkie with him, Baldwin had another one at the Motor Lodge, and McCord and Barker carried additional ones.

Reaching the door that leads from the garage to the office building's stairwell, the five men were stunned to find that the tape had been removed. The door was locked. Virgílio Gonzalez, the locksmith, was told by Barker to pick the lock, and he was left alone to do the job. McCord went back to Baldwin's room across the street. Barker, Sturgis, and Martinez returned to Room 214. It was a contretemps, and the men were quite nervous. About 1:30 A.M., Gonzalez radioed that he succeeded in jimmying the garage door. McCord, Barker, Sturgis, and Martinez rejoined him, and they walked up the office building stairwell, again taping the garage doors as well as the door leading from the sixth-floor landing on the stairs to the sixth-floor lobby. (Gonzalez again had to use his locksmith tools to unlock the doors.) Once in the lobby, Gonzalez broke the lock on the glass doors leading to the Democratic National Committee's suite, and the raiders moved into the Youth Division office and began going through the files. It is not clear why this was the first task they undertook.

A few minutes later, Frank Wills, the guard, was back in the garage checking the doors. Finding the doors taped again, this time he called the police. At 1:52 A.M., three Metropolitan Police plainclothesmen, dressed in casual clothes, received their dispatcher's call in an unmarked patrol car and raced to the Watergate. They checked with Wills, saw the tape on the garage doors, and proceeded to inspect the office building from the bottom floor up. Baldwin, who was watching the Watergate from his room across the street, saw lights go on on the eighth floor, two floors above where the raiders were at work. He radioed this information, which was received over Hunt's as well as the raiders' walkie-talkies. The answer came from Hunt, who assured Baldwin that this was a routine guard check. A few minutes later, Baldwin spotted two men in casual clothes, one of them with his pistol drawn, on the sixth-floor terrace. Baldwin radioed Hunt in Room 214 that real trouble appeared to be developing because they were armed, informally dressed men on the sixth floor of the Watergate office building. The raiders were wearing business suits and, therefore, Baldwin became alarmed when he saw men in slacks and windbreakers. Baldwin's recollection is that Hunt suddenly sounded frantic over the walkie-talkie.

The three policemen who were now inside the Democratic offices detected movement behind a glass partition. One of the officers, gun in hand, ordered the raiders to come out with their hands up. They still had their rubber gloves on. Baldwin said later in a newspaper interview that he heard McCord's choked voice over the walkie-talkie saying, "They got us." Hunt radioed Baldwin that he would come right over to the Motor Lodge. With Liddy a step behind him, Howard Hunt jumped into a car, made a U-turn on Virginia Avenue, and pulled up at the Howard Johnson Motor Lodge. Liddy vanished. Hunt went up to Baldwin's room alone, repeating to himself, "What's happened? What's happened?"

After he composed himself, Hunt telephoned Michael Douglas Caddy, a lawyer with whom he was acquainted from the Mullen firm, to say that he was on the way to his apartment. He ordered Baldwin to pack up all the electronic equipment in the room and take it to McCord's house in Rockville, in suburban Maryland. McCord's pickup truck, which Baldwin drove to Rockville, contained tape recorders, two electric typewriters belonging to Howard Hunt, and electronic gear removed from the Motor Lodge room. Hunt then rushed downstairs, got into his car, and drove to the Mullen company offices on Pennsylvania Avenue. From there, he telephoned Clara, Barker's wife, in Miami, according to one of the versions surrounding the confused events of that dawn. The other version is that Caddy had instructions to telephone Mrs. Barker by 2 A.M., if something had gone wrong and he had not heard from Hunt. Caddy, apparently, was not familiar with Hunt's plan—except that he had been told to call Miami —and the idea seemed to be that Mrs. Barker would then try to locate a Washington lawyer by telephone to deal with an emergency. It is somewhat puzzling that in all his careful planning, Hunt had not taken the precaution of having a Committee to Re-

Elect lawyer standing by in case of need, even if he were not told why. Perhaps Hunt was overconfident. From the Mullen company, Hunt went to his office in the Executive Office Building, next to the White House, and removed some cash from his safe. Then he went to Caddy's apartment and made a series of telephone calls to locate a criminal lawyer. Caddy was not a criminal specialist. Subsequently, Hunt telephoned Liddy, who had gone home, to tell him that a Joseph Rafferty had agreed to try to bail out the Watergate Five.

It was morning on Sunday, June 18, when Howard Hunt—red-eyed, exhausted, and highly nervous—reached his home in Potomac. Dorothy was in Europe on a vacation with their daughter Kevan. They had dined with an old friend in Paris the previous evening. But the three other Hunt children were at home. Hunt slept most of the morning, unaware of the incredible magnitude of the night's disaster. He evidently assumed that McCord, as well as Barker and his team, would remain silent and no connection would ever be traced between the raiders and himself, to say nothing of the White House. He could not imagine that the events of the past few hours marked the beginning of the greatest political scandal of the century in the United States and that he would soon become one of its chief public actors.

.What Hunt did not know was that after arresting the five raiders in the Watergate office, the police had gone to Rooms 214 and 314, which the Miami men had occupied since their arrival. One reason why the police went to the hotel may have been the fact that the raiders had on them $1300 in consecutively numbered $100 bills. In the rooms, the police found another $3200, again in consecutively numbered $100 bills. They also discovered Barker's little black address book and Martinez's portable flip-to-open telephone directory. Hunt's home number was listed in both. Also, in Barker's address book, an entry said "H.H.," followed by a dash and the initials "W.H." (White House) and

Hunt's telephone number in the Executive Office Building where a room had now been assigned to him on the fifth floor. I had an opportunity to examine Barker's address book and, on one of the pages, there appeared this scrawl: *"Yo soy Macho! Avanti!"* (I am Macho! Onward!)

Although they went through the address books, the police, all that day and for a while longer, had no idea of the real nature of the case they had on their hands. The FBI, which entered the case on Monday, only established the connection with Hunt a few days later.

Early on Sunday afternoon, a friend from my Cuban days called me at my Washington home to ask whether I realized the meaning of Watergate. I had superficially read a newspaper account of the burglary and had drawn no particular conclusions from it. My friend asked me whether the name "Eduardo" meant anything to me. I said it did not. Later that day, I met with my friend and he refreshed my memory. Eduardo was the man I had known casually in Miami in 1961, during the preparations for the Bay of Pigs. "It is Eduardo who is behind this whole business," my friend told me. Eduardo's real name was E. Howard Hunt, Jr., and he worked at the White House. I suspect that I may have been the first person to alert Hunt to the fact that knowledge existed that he had some involvement with the Watergate burglary. Of course, I did not know at the time that Hunt's initials and the White House telephone number were listed in Barker's address book, but what I did know from my friend was that Barker, identified in the Sunday newspaper accounts, had worked for Hunt in the 1961 CIA operation. Having gone to my newspaper office to write a story about the break-in, I looked up Hunt's number in the telephone directory as well as his listing in *Who's Who*. It is a professional habit to look people's names up in *Who's Who*, particularly when one knows them to be in some way identified with the White House. Then, because I did not want my own name to surface prematurely in the handling of the story, I asked one of my colleagues at the office to call Hunt. He dialed the number, and Hunt himself answered. My colleague asked him whether Hunt knew anything about the Watergate events. Hunt said he did not. Then my colleague, trying out a ploy we had worked out, said "But Macho Barker says he knows you." Hunt slammed down the receiver. He had panicked, probably assuming (wrongly) that Barker had told all to the police.

Reconstructing his steps, I found out that Hunt arrived at his Washington bank, one of the branches of the Riggs National Bank, at precisely 9:00 A.M., on Monday, June 19, just as it opened for business. He went to his safe-deposit box and withdrew a certain amount of cash. Bank records show that Hunt went to his safe-deposit box, but of course they do not show what he took out. My own surmise is that Hunt was alarmed because someone—he thought it was the police and not just someone on my newspaper—was aware of a link between him and Barker. He may have still expected some protection from Barker and the other raiders although he feared they might have named him, but he did not know what *we* would do with this information. For that matter, we did not know either. Second-hand information that Barker knew Eduardo and that Eduardo, who was Hunt, was behind the Watergate raid, was not yet sufficient data to write a responsible newspaper story.

Inevitably, the FBI was presently able to link Howard Hunt with the Barker team and the White House. It also discovered that Republican money was "laundered" through Mexico and Barker's Miami bank account.

That Hunt's initials and White House phone number appeared in Barker's address book was the fatal slip in the whole carefully concocted operation. Why did Hunt not check before the raid on what his men had in their pockets? Or if he had and found an address book, why would he let Barker leave it in the hotel room? The address book, besides Hunt's number, had the names and Miami telephone numbers of a large number of Cubans with CIA connections, including Captain Artime. Hunt also committed another indiscretion, inexcusable in a professional intelligence officer. When McCord was searched, a check for a small amount made out to the Lakewood Country Club (to which McCord belongs) and signed by Hunt was found in his possession.

There is one more possible indiscretion, if not sloppiness, committed by Hunt. During the Senate Select Committee hearings, Robert C. Mardian, formerly the head of the Justice Department's Internal Security Division, testified that he was informed by Magruder that the CIA had provided false papers to the Watergate raiders. We know that Hunt carried two sets of false papers —one in the name of Edward J. Hamilton and the other in the name of Edward Warren—given him by the CIA in August 1971. If Hunt also asked the CIA to forge documents for McCord and the Miami team, then both he and the Agency were guilty of dangerous foolishness.

In any event, Hunt was immensely concerned about his situation. On Monday, after taking money from his safe-deposit box, he flew from Washington to the John F. Kennedy International Airport in New York. He spent the night at an airport motel. Witnesses testified that two days after the break-in—on Monday— Chuck Colson had phoned Hunt to tell him to get out of the United States, but his colleagues at the White House cautioned Colson, according to testimony, that Hunt's going abroad, if discovered, might create even greater suspicions in the Watergate case. Hunt, after all, had worked in the White House. Colson tried to countermand his instructions but could no longer contact Hunt.

There are two versions concerning Hunt's steps during the week following the Watergate burglary. One is that Hunt flew to Madrid but returned to Washington when he, too, became convinced that sooner or later his absence from the country could embarrass the White House. He may have stayed just one or two days in Spain. But there is no corroboration for this version. The other version is that Hunt flew to Los Angeles, where he remained hidden for a number of days at the home of a lawyer whom he had known in the past as a CIA officer. In either case, there is no question that Hunt spent a number of days in the Los Angeles area.

On June 23, Hunt telephoned Bob Bennett, his boss at the Mullen firm, from a public telephone somewhere in the United States. He asked Bennett to contact the White House and request that a lawyer be found for him. Within days, Hunt returned to Washington, and it was announced that William O. Bittman, a well-known Washington lawyer and former Justice Department prosecutor, had been retained as Hunt's attorney. Bittman had gained fame as a prosecutor in cases which led to the conviction of James R. Hoffa, former head of the Teamsters' Union, and Robert (Bobby) Baker, a one-time protégé of President Johnson. Hunt was interviewed by FBI agents at his Potomac home. He told them precious little.

Howard Hunt's personal behavior after his return to Washington tells a strange story. It is a story of deceit, lies, blackmail, and disloyalty toward virtually everybody with whom he had been associated.

On July 20, Hunt began to threaten the White House with public disclosure of his other secret activities in the Special Investigative Unit unless he was paid off. Hunt is said to have sent a message, saying "the Writer has a manuscript of a play to sell," via Caddy, the lawyer whom he visited the night of the break-in, to be passed on to the White House. Caddy relayed the word to Paul O'Brien, an attorney for the Committee to Re-Elect, who, in turn, passed it on to John Dean.

Hunt's message apparently was understood quite well at the White House, because large payments began to be made to him almost immediately for his and his family's expenses as well as for Bittman's fees. To be sure, Hunt had lost his income from the Mullen company, for he never again went back to work there. His continued employment there was in any case highly unlikely, even if he had reported for duty. Bennett made that clear. Dorothy Hunt lost her part-time job at the Spanish Embassy, following *The New York Times*' publication of a story I had written about her work there. Hunt, of course, still had his CIA retirement pay, but he was evidently after bigger stakes. Again it was his insatiable desire for money.

The fact that large payments were made by the White House to Hunt seems to support the idea that the White House Special Investigative Unit had engaged in activities that are still secret. It appeared that the White House may still have an interest in protecting Hunt for what the President has described as "national security" reasons. One may theorize that some kind of an agreement exists between Hunt and his former White House superiors that he will maintain his silence about certain top-secret projects, despite his public complaints that they let him down. It may be further theorized that these payments continued throughout 1973. Nixon himself said that he was apprised in March 1973 that Hunt was demanding $120,000 in fresh money to keep from revealing information that he, Hunt, believed to be extremely damaging to the administration.

James McCord, who never belonged to the Special Unit, said in a memorandum submitted to the Senate Watergate investigating committee and federal prosecutors in the case on May 8, 1973, that the FBI and the CIA had been prevented from properly investigating Watergate on White House orders. "E. Howard Hunt has additional information relevant to the above. Hunt stated to me on more than one occasion in the latter part of 1972, that he, Hunt, had information in his possession which 'would be sufficient to impeach the President.' " (Late in August 1973, new information was developed that Hunt had maintained contacts with a senior Secret Service agent in Miami sometime in 1971 for reasons that were not immediately clear.) "In addition," McCord said, "Mrs. E. Howard Hunt, on or about November, 1972, in a personal conversation with me, stated that E. Howard Hunt had just dictated a three-page letter which Hunt's attorney, William O. Bittman, had read to Kenneth Parkinson, the attorney for the Committee to Re-Elect the President, in which letter Hunt purportedly threatened to 'blow the White House out of the water.' Mrs. Hunt at this point in her conversation with me, also repeated the statement which she, too, had made before, which was that E. Howard Hunt had information which could impeach the President."

In September 1972, Hunt testified before a federal grand jury in Washington. He freely admitted his part in the Watergate break-in, but volunteered no information concerning the 1971 raid on Dr. Fielding's office in Los Angeles or the forgery of Vietnam cables intended to blacken John F. Kennedy's reputation. Federal prosecutors, ignorant of these matters, did not question him about anything except the Watergate burglary. The existence of the Special Unit was not known to them at the time.

Along with Liddy and the "Watergate Five," Hunt was indicted on September 15. His indictment on six counts was based principally on his role in the Watergate burglary. When Hunt and his associates came to court in January 1973, the judge was unaware that there was much more to the case than just a conspiracy to commit political espionage through the Watergate break-ins, although newspapers insisted that this was part of a wider operation directed from "high up."

Since Ehrlichman, Krogh, and Young as former Presidential aides are protected in all their testimony by executive privilege invoked by Nixon and accepted by the Senate Select Committee on matters pertaining to national security, only Hunt and Liddy could conceivably tell the full story of the Special Unit's activities. Testifying under special immunity from further prosecution before grand jurors in Washington and Los Angeles in 1973, after his sentencing, Hunt only then disclosed the other aspects of his activities. He admitted that he was involved in the Ellsberg raid and the Vietnamese papers forgery, after word about these projects leaked out through other channels. But even in April, he volunteered nothing else of importance. Evidently, he was keeping his end of what apparently was a blackmail bargain. He was the "Writer" ready to sell the manuscript of his "play" to the highest bidder. Liddy, on the other hand, has maintained absolute silence on every subject as of the time this is being written in late August 1973.

A rough estimate in mid-1973 was that Hunt collected more than $200,000 in payments from the White House and the Re-Election Committee, beginning in July 1971. Until December 1972, the money was usually given to Dorothy Hunt by Tony Ulasewicz, the White House investigator. After her death, payments were handled through Bittman and other channels. But in mid-August 1973, Bittman withdrew as Hunt's attorney without any explanation, to be replaced by another Washington lawyer, Sidney Sachs. Some investigators believe that Bittman had collected over $90,000 in legal fees by the time he withdrew from the case. Ulasewicz testified earlier that he alone paid Bittman $25,000 in fees, leaving the money in a brown envelope in a telephone booth in the lobby of the attorney's office building. (In those days, by the way, Hunt and Mrs. Hunt were called in the White House the "Writer" and the "Writer's Wife.")

Between his indictment and the trial, Hunt, as were the others, was free on bail. He used his time to protect his flanks in a variety of ways—the money demands conveyed to the "higher-ups" by Dorothy and Bittman was one—and to complete his latest novel. On January 18, 1973, a few days after pleading guilty, he went to San Francisco to appear on the television program *Firing Line,* moderated by his old friend Bill Buckley. This was Hunt's only public appearance since Watergate. Hunt was cool and composed as he sat before the cameras, dapper in a dark suit and conservative necktie. His first words on the program showed his anger at the government and the CIA, as he told Buckley that he considered that the official disclosure of his Agency past was a "unilateral abrogation by the government of a commitment that we entered upon my retirement from the Central Intelligence Agency." Defiantly, but less accurately, he also said, "I was never a fugitive."

Under Buckley's tough questioning, Hunt acknowledged that the Watergate operation was conducted "in the spirit of a CIA action." Buckley, himself a one-time CIA agent, was seeking to establish the rather fundamental point that "lifelong experience . . . with the CIA teaches a person to forget about the legal impediments that lie between him and the accomplishment of a mission that he seeks to achieve." At one point this dialogue developed:

BUCKLEY: . . . If one spends twenty years working for the CIA, is it likely that on returning to one's own country one has so much absorbed the ethos of the CIA that one tends to go after what it is that one wants and to consider local legislation that stands in the way as sort of irrelevant?

HUNT: If one even were to consider local legislation, it would not be illegal under United States law, for example, for CIA to mount an entry operation in Ottawa or Fort Erie, Canada, the other side of the Peace Bridge. But here we have a geographical distinction. We would not be guilty under United States law of, let's say, a second-degree burglary charge by the United States for an operation that we conducted in Canada or in Mexico. We *would* be, were it conducted in Florida or Texas or Southern California.

Rereading the transcript of the *Firing Line* program in the light of knowledge developed in subsequent months, one is inevitably intrigued by Hunt's discussion of hypothetical operations "in Canada or Mexico." There have been other suggestions that the Special Unit mounted operations in Mexico. There is the fact that Hunt did obtain a Mexican tourism card as "Edward J. Hamilton," the identity given him by the CIA in 1971. And there is the long and contradictory record of testimony, as well as internal CIA and White House documents, as to whether FBI investigations in Mexico of some aspects of Watergate might endanger the Agency's covert operations there. This record suggests strongly that the White House exercised maximum pressure to prevail on the CIA to declare that FBI investigations in Mexico *would* be detrimental. McCord has written that "the FBI was apparently proscribed at every turn. . . . Even routine investigative efforts were suppressed. . . . The question then is: who kept the wraps on the FBI in its investigation of the Watergate case?" So among the many unanswered questions about the White House Special Unit, there is the one as to whether, indeed, it was involved in covert foreign operations that were kept hidden even from the CIA. Is this among the secrets still kept by Hunt and Liddy?

While Howard Hunt continued his apparent blackmail activities—and kept getting paid—he also became part of a major effort by the White House to implicate the CIA in Watergate. President Nixon acknowledged in May 1973 that at the outset of the Watergate investigation, he received the impression that the Agency might indeed have organized the break-in. The initial effort to implicate the CIA died down during the autumn of 1972 but was revived early in December, with Hunt playing a major role in the revival.

There is no evidence to pinpoint the source of the new efforts to embarrass the CIA. But in his memorandum to the Senate Committee and federal prosecutors, McCord insisted that enormous pressure was exercised by Hunt and others in December to establish a line of defense in the approaching Watergate trial that the burglary had been staged and orchestrated by the CIA. McCord said that he resisted this plan. Barker told him that as a result, "Hunt was very bitter about it. . . . Hunt's bitterness was later revealed early in the trial when the Cubans advised that Hunt had said that I 'was responsible for our being in the plight we were in for not going along with the CIA thing.' "

McCord said that, "Even if it meant my freedom, I would not turn on the organization that had employed me for nineteen years, and wrongly deal such a damaging blow that it would take years for it to recover from it. . . . I believe that organization to be one of the finest organizations of any kind in the world, and would not let anyone wrongly lay the operation at the feet of the CIA." For months, McCord kept writing letters to CIA Director Helms warning him of such an intrigue.

It is, of course, possible that McCord was being self-serving. But the record shows that it was McCord's letter to Judge John J. Sirica in March 1973, charging perjury in the January trial, that made it possible to reopen the Watergate investigation. McCord told the Judge that the Watergate operation was conducted by Hunt and Liddy under the auspices of the White House and the Re-Election Committee. He provided facts that blew the Watergate story wide open. It was, it developed, a scandal of extraordinary proportions.

McCord said that he was convinced that the White House was behind "the idea and ploy which had been presented" to blame the CIA and "that the White House was turning ruthless and would do whatever was politically expedient at any one particular point in time to accomplish its own ends." Subsequent testimony confirmed that Howard Hunt had, indeed, decided to turn against the CIA. It is unknown whether this was a personal decision based on a sense of bitterness against the Agency he had served for nearly twenty-three years, or whether this was part of a larger understanding with the White House.

McCord, and he is not alone in this, believes that the anti-CIA conspiracy related to a wider White House plan to make the Agency more subservient to the National Security Council and to weaken it in favor of the Pentagon's Defense Intelligence Agency. Many key people in the intelligence community suspect that Richard Helms, then Director of Central Intelligence, was the White House's chief target and that early in 1973 he accepted the post of Ambassador to Iran only with the greatest reluctance. (As I have mentioned earlier, the White House increasingly resented the CIA's intellectual independence and its disagreements with the National Security Council.) It is hard to imagine what else could have been gained by so damaging the CIA's reputation. But as Senate testimony has shown, the White House also developed an almost paranoid distrust of the FBI and the Secret Service.

Another strange situation involving Hunt in late 1972 was the removal of certain papers from his safe in the Executive Office Building. This allegedly highly sensitive material was turned over to L. Patrick Gray III, then the FBI's Acting Director, who burned it in December at his Connecticut home after reading the contents. Gray had insisted earlier that he had not read the papers before destroying them, but later he changed his testimony.

There are reasons to believe, however, that one or possibly two duplicate sets of this material were in Hunt's possession—and this would make sense. If Hunt was engaged in heavy blackmail, it would be imperative for him to be able to produce documentation of whatever disclosures he might want to make. His CIA background, if nothing else, would lead him to take such precautions. The sensitivity of the material in Hunt's safe was emphasized in John Dean's testimony, alleging that Ehrlichman ordered him to "deep-six" the documents—to dump them in the Potomac River. Ehrlichman said he never made such a suggestion, but the fact remains that Pat Gray did burn the documents. McCord has said, "Mrs. Hunt told me in late July 1972 that her husband also had to dispose of incriminating material at their residence. Would such materials have led to the Ellsberg break-in and other 'plumbers' operations' of the White House? My guess is yes."

It may well be that someone suspected that Hunt had duplicate sets of the documents at home. According to reliable information in my possession, federal agents armed with a search warrant went painstakingly through Hunt's residence in December 1972, but found nothing. My informants also suggest that Hunt turned one set of the documents over to a friend for safekeeping. This may have been the second set, if there were only two, or the third if Hunt did dispose of the second. The identity of Hunt's friend, the one who may hold the last existing set of documents, is unknown, but it is believed to be a person who lives in Washington's Virginia suburbs, possibly in Arlington or Alexandria.

On December 8, 1972, Dorothy Hunt died in the crash of a United Airlines plane making its final approach to Chicago. Investigators found on her body $10,585, mostly in $100 bills. Sabotage was charged but never proven. But it was a week after the crash that federal agents appeared at Hunt's home with the search warrant.

Hunt, Liddy, McCord, and the four men from Miami were brought to the United States District Court in Washington early in January 1973. Five pleaded guilty, including Hunt; Liddy and McCord, who did not, were found guilty after the jury trial.

When time came for sentencing on March 23, 1973, McCord submitted his letter to Judge Sirica claiming that "there was political pressure applied to the defendants to plead guilty and remain silent: perjury occurred during the trial in matters highly material to the very structure, orientation and impact of the Government's case, and to the motivation and intent of the defendants; others involved in the Watergate operation were not identified during the trial, when they could have been. . . . The Watergate operation was not a CIA operation. The Cubans may have been misled by others in believing that it was a CIA operation. I know for a fact that it was not."

Only McCord knows why he decided to tell the truth. His claim that he did so out of loyalty to the CIA may well be the truth. His revelations of perjury during the January trial have created a situation in which his case may have to be reviewed. In fact, he was the only one of the Watergate defendants not sentenced on March 23.

Howard Hunt, however, is another story. In attempting to comprehend his complex personality, it may be pertinent to study the statement he made to the Court before sentencing:

I stand before you, a man convicted, first by the press, then by my own admissions, freely made even at the beginning of my trial. For twenty-six years I served my country honorably and with devotion: first as a Naval officer in the wartime North Atlantic, then as an Air Force officer in China. And, finally, as an officer of the Central Intelligence Agency combating our country's enemies abroad.

In my entire life, I was never charged with a crime, much less convicted of one. Since the 17th of June, 1972, I lost my employment, then my beloved wife, both in consequence of my involvement in the Watergate affair. Today, I stand before the bar of justice alone, nearly friendless, ridiculed, disgraced, destroyed as a man.

These have been a few of the many tragic consequences of my participation in the Watergate affair, and they have been visited upon me in overwhelming measure. What I did was wrong, unquestionably wrong in the eyes of the law, and I can accept that. For the last eight months, I have suffered an ever-deepening consciousness of guilt, or responsibility for my acts, and of the drastic penalties they entailed. I pray, however, that this Court—and the American people—can accept my statement today that my motives were not evil.

The offenses I have freely admitted are the first in a life of blameless and honorable conduct. As a man already destroyed by the consequences of his acts, I can represent no threat to our society, now or at any conceivable future time. And as to the function of deterrence, Your Honor, the Watergate case has been so publicized, that I believe it fair to say that the American public knows that political offenses are not to be tolerated by our society within our democratic system.

The American public knows also that, because of what I did, I have lost virtually everything that I cherished in life—my wife, my job, my reputation. Surely, these tragic consequences will serve as an effective deterrent to anyone else who might contemplate engaging in a similar activity.

The offenses to which I pleaded guilty even before trial began were not crimes of violence. To be sure, they were an affront to the state, but not to the body of a man or to his property. The real victims of the Watergate conspiracy, Your Honor, as it has turned out, are the conspirators themselves. But there are other prospective victims.

Your Honor, I am the father of four children, the youngest a boy of nine. Had my wife and I not lost our employment because of Watergate involvement, she would not have sought investment security for our family in Chicago, where she was killed last December. My children's knowledge of the reason for her death is ineradicable—as is mine. Four children without a mother. I ask that they not lose their father, as well.

Your Honor, I cannot believe the end of Justice would be well served by incarcerating me. To do so would add four more victims to the disastrous train of events in which I was involved. I say to you, in all candor, that my family desperately needs me at this time. My problems are unique and real, and Your Honor knows what they are. My probation officer has discussed them with me at some length.

I have spent almost an entire lifetime helping and serving my

country, in war and peace. I am the one who now needs help.
Throughout the civilized world, we are renowned for our American
system of justice. Especially honored is our judicial concept of justice
tempered with mercy. Mercy, Your Honor, not vengeance and reprisal,
as in some lands. It is this revered tradition of mercy that I ask Your
Honor to remember while you ponder my fate.

It is an extraordinary statement. In it, Howard Hunt asked
the court to look at him as the Howard Hunt before Watergate—
the man who served his country for twenty-six years and whose
first and only offense, as he put it, "were not crimes of violence"
and not an affront "to the body of a man or to his property."

I used the word "deceit" in speaking of Hunt's attitudes after
the Watergate burglary. I believe that Hunt's plea in court bears
out the use of this harsh word. When he was addressing the court,
neither the judge nor the public knew of the burglary at Dr.
Fielding's office, the contrived political demonstrations in which
people were struck, the forging of documents to destroy the
honor of a dead President, the blackmailing of the White House,
and the effort, possibly orchestrated with others, to throw the
whole responsibility for Watergate on the CIA and thus assure a
continued cover-up for the White House.

Did Howard Hunt assume that his acts *before* Watergate
and his subsequent personal manipulations would never come
to light? If so, he was willfully deceiving the judge before whom
he was pleading for justice tempered with mercy.

Grave questions arise as to why Hunt acted as he did. Was it
his belief that his successful blackmail of the Government would
prevent these deeds from becoming public? Hunt has denied from
his prison cell that the money he had been receiving constitutes
blackmail. Instead, he says, it was for "maintenance payments"
and lawyers' fees. He told a *Time* magazine interviewer that this
was "the same sort of arrangement that the CIA gives its agents

who are captured. . . . We had no silence to sell." He said it costs him up to $1500 each day he makes a legal appearance.

It is important to bear some dates in mind. Hunt addressed the court—evidently confident that all of his past would never be revealed—on the same day that McCord wrote Judge Sirica charging perjury in the trial and thus, in effect, reopening the Watergate case. Hunt obviously did not know of this when he spoke in court. In any event, Judge Sirica imposed a thirty-five year "provisional" sentence on him, defined so as to encourage him to change his mind about keeping silent.

According to President Nixon's statement of August 15, 1973, Nixon found out about the Los Angeles break-in on March 17 —six days before Hunt addressed the court—and there are no reasons to believe that he was aware of the President's new knowledge. The chances are that Hunt was also unaware that on March 21, *two days* before he addressed the court, Nixon was informed of his blackmail activities. They had been covered up by others in the White House. By the same token, Hunt could not have foreseen that in mid-April, some three weeks later, the Justice Department and the federal grand jury would reopen the case, largely on the basis of McCord's revelations, and, among other things, bring out the Ellsberg matter.

But again, there is a perturbing phrase in President Nixon's August statement:

On April 18, I learned that the Justice Department had interrogated or was going to interrogate Mr. Hunt about this [Los Angeles] break-in. I was gravely concerned that other activities of the Special Investigative Unit might be disclosed, because I knew this could seriously injure the national security. Consequently, I directed Mr. Peterson [the Assistant Attorney General] to stick to the Watergate investigation and stay out of national security matters. On April 25, Attorney General Kleindienst came to me and urged that the fact of the break-in should be disclosed to the court, despite the fact that, since no evidence had been obtained, the law did not clearly require it. I concurred, and authorized him to report the break-in to Judge [Matthew] Byrne [conducting Ellsberg's trial in Los Angeles].

Hunt's testimony before the reconvened grand jury in Washington during April helps somewhat to explain the Presidential apprehensions. Speaking of the Special Unit, he told the grand jury:

The operational direction of that group was provided by Mr. Egil Krogh. . . . It became known to Mr. Liddy and myself, and I believe it must have been Mr. Krogh who told us, that there was an intense amount of interest in Dr. Ellsberg. Dr. Ellsberg had been indicted not long before, and the White House had been receiving, I believe on a daily basis, reports from the FBI and other agencies of the government. I think there would be weekly summaries and compilations, some of them rather elaborately indexed. I was given access to all this material on an absolutely routine basis. I became very familiar with the case itself. At that time, as I understood it, there was some concern in the White House about the appropriateness of seeing the prosecution actually take place, with regard to Dr. Ellsberg and his associates, and I shared that concern, my own feeling being that he would probably become a martyr, in looking at things politically, and I felt that it was a poor judgment to draw. . . .

I believe Mr. Krogh, who was the lawyer, suggested that it would be well if something could—if some way could be found whereby a judgment could be made on Ellsberg in regard to his prosecutability. To that end, extracts were made of material dealing with Dr. Ellsberg's rather peculiar background, and we read these excerpts and concluded that the best instant sources of a full read-out, or a reasonably full read-out on Dr. Ellsberg, would be through whatever files the psychiatrist had been maintaining on him during the period that Dr. Ellsberg was under analysis. I don't know who mentioned the possibility of a bag-job on the psychiatrist's office, but in any event, it became a topic of low-key conversation around the office. . . . There came a time shortly thereafter when it was suggested that perhaps the unit, which has been popularly described as the "plumbers" in the press, but which was never so called during incumbency, might be able to undertake such an operation on its own. To that end, Mr. Liddy and I were authorized to fly out to the West Coast, Los Angeles. . . . We were authorized to make a preliminary vulnerability and feasibility study for such an operation.

Discussing the forgery of the Vietnam documents, Hunt told the grand jury that having been unable to obtain the necessary material from the Pentagon and the CIA, and not enough from the State Department, he reported this to Chuck Colson, with whom he had been discussing the project. Colson, Hunt said, asked him, "Well, what kind of material have you dug up on the files that would indicate Kennedy's complicity?" Hunt replied that he showed him "three or four cables that indicated that they had pretty close to pulled the trigger against Premier [sic] Diem's head, but it did not say so in so many words. . . . Inferentially, one could say that it was a high degree of Administration complicity in the actual assassination of Diem and his brother."

Hunt said that Colson remarked, "This isn't good enough. Do you think that you could improve on them?" Hunt replied, "I probably could, but not without technical assistance." He told Colson, "After all, I had been given some training in my past CIA career to do just this sort of thing, and have done it successfully on numerous occasions, floating forged newspaper accounts, telegrams, that sort of thing." But Colson told him, "We won't be able to give you any technical help. This is too hot. See what you can do on your own." Hunt then went on to describe how he forged the telegrams with a razor blade, typewriter, and Xerox machine.

In an affidavit to the grand jury, Egil Krogh said that in July 1971 he had been given "oral instructions" by Ehrlichman to begin "a special national security project" to deal with disclosures of classified documents. He said that the Special Unit developed information that made it "imperative to ascertain whether the unauthorized disclosure of the Pentagon Papers was (a) an individual act, (b) the act of a small group, or (c) the result of a wider conspiracy to engage in espionage. . . . The affiant received information suggesting that Dr. Ellsberg did not act alone."

Krogh said that he had been "informed repeatedly during the months of July and August 1971 of the extreme threat perceived to be developing by high government officials, because of the possibility of further unauthorized disclosure as to the capacity of the United States government to conduct its foreign affairs and protect its national security." Krogh explained the need to obtain a psychological profile of Dr. Ellsberg and said that "general authorization to engage in covert activity to obtain a psychological history or ascertain associates of Dr. Fielding was thereafter given to the Special Unit by John D. Ehrlichman." Krogh also said that Hunt and Liddy had recommended that a new attempt be made to obtain the Ellsberg file.

The record shows Hunt's extreme tension during the period preceding and following the trial and the sentencing. With a touch of desperation, he repeatedly tried to contact Chuck Colson, but found no response. Then he wrote him a letter requesting a meeting to discuss his problems. After serious consideration, the decision was made at the White House that Colson might see Bittman, Hunt's lawyer, but not Hunt himself. Accounts of this meeting indicate that Bittman again raised the question of executive clemency for Hunt. Nixon was to say later that although such an approach was made on Hunt's behalf, neither Colson nor anyone else ever promised clemency.

But after new disclosures in April and May 1973 and after his testimony before grand juries in Washington and Los Angeles, as well as before a number of Congressional Subcommittees and to investigators for the Special Watergate Prosecutor, Archibald Cox, Howard Hunt seemed to become somewhat more relaxed. To be sure, he was shuttled from jail to jail. His first stay after sentencing was at the appalling District of Columbia jail. There, he charged, some of his papers were stolen. He was moved to the federal prison at Danbury, Connecticut, and then to the Alexandria, Virginia, jail and back again to Danbury.

Early in June, after testifying before the grand jury in Los Angeles, Hunt told newsmen, "I am not Cinna the Conspirator. I am Cinna the Poet." Hunt was referring to a scene from *Julius Caesar*, after Mark Antony has inflamed the mob to revenge Caesar's murder, and a poet named Cinna enters the scene; the enraged mob kills him because he has the same name as one of the conspirators. Hunt seemed to be comparing himself to a poet who was an innocent bystander, a victim of a politician's clever oratory and of a bloody-minded public determined to get revenge. This was Howard Hunt the classicist, who would turn to Pliny the Elder for epigraphs for his spy novels.

When he was not shuttling from hearing to hearing and prison to prison, Hunt has been reading and writing heavily. He occasionally received visitors at Danbury. Bill Buckley, his best friend, said that Hunt would telephone him every once in a while from Danbury to chat. Sometimes, Buckley said, "he would be up, some days he would be down."

After six months in prison, Hunt has lost about twenty-five pounds, and because of a slight stroke limps a bit when he walks. Federal investigators who have repeatedly interviewed him say that he has become a "pathetic" figure. One who got to know him well believes that Hunt's last ounce of self-esteem goes into verbal fencing with his questioners. "It's his final challenge," he said.

Prison life was demoralizing for Hunt. When he was transported from Danbury to make legal appearances, his legs were placed in irons and his wrists manacled to a chain around his waist. His prison work was at the library, but he complained that in the absence of a typewriter, he could not seriously work on a new book. So he spent most of his free time answering letters and scribbling on a pad. He was bitter about everything and everybody. In August, he told a magazine interviewer that "We were just legmen . . . yet we're the only ones who have suffered from it so far. . . . I can't for the life of me understand. Here are the prime conspirators walking around on the streets, free on bond. But there's no end in sight for me. I think it's ironic and inequitable." Hunt also claimed that the discovery of the Watergate break-in may have been deliberate: "Too many fishy things occurred."

Possibly Hunt is right, and the Watergate disaster was actually planned from the White House—though not the consequences it eventually had. There is a growing school of thought in Washington that "powerful men" in the White House had wanted to see a relatively minor scandal occur that would victimize John Mitchell politically, sacrificing McCord and the Cuban-Americans in the process. The reasoning is that the White House and "1701," that is, the Committee to Re-Elect, were engaged in mortal combat to gain Nixon's favor. If this theory is accurate, then someone in the White House might have tipped off either the Watergate building guard or the police—or both—so that the raiders would be caught. What nobody could predict, including Hunt, was that through his last-minute carelessness the police would find his compromising White House telephone number on Barker and the check on McCord, thus establishing the link between them and Howard Hunt and consequently the White House. Mitchell was destroyed—but so were Hunt and Liddy.

Hunt still prefers to address his public through his books. Since his 1972 misfortunes, he completed his latest novel, *The Berlin Ending*. It is perhaps the strangest of all of his books. His publisher appears to have reached the same conclusion, because the blurb on the book's jacket has this to say: "What sort of man is Howard Hunt? . . . What the CREEP (Committee to Re-Elect the President) conspirators sought to lay bare in Daniel Ellsberg, Howard Hunt unwittingly lays bare in himself. . . ."

Briefly, the theme of *Berlin Ending* is that the West German Foreign Minister, whom Hunt calls Klaus Johann Werber, but who unquestionably is Willy Brandt, is a secret Communist agent. Hunt calls him an "Agent of Influence." He serves the Soviet Union under the guise of being a peacemaker aspiring for the Nobel Prize and the post of Secretary General of the United Nations. There is the usual Huntian mix of politics, sex, violence, alcohol, and undercover work. That Hunt really had Willy Brandt in mind when he wrote his novel was suggested by the fact that from prison he sent his New York editor a newspaper picture of Brandt with Leonid Brezhnev with this notation in his handwriting, "Here's the dirty dog with his master."

Most revealing is the book's final page. There, an Israeli intelligence officers tells the novel's hero, Neal Thorpe, "Werber was always the Soviet's man. And they take care of their own.'

" 'Unlike CIA,' Thorpe said thinly. 'Damn them, too.' "

Z

How does one explain Howard Hunt? In a way, he comes across as the central figure in a *roman à clef* that he might have written. Except that he is a real man in real life and the *clef* has not yet been found and perhaps never will be.

The temptation is to say the obvious: that somewhere along

the tortuous path of his life Howard Hunt has lost the precious distinction between fantasy and reality. Another temptation is to declare simply that he was the product of the Cold War and the special mentality that comes from a lifetime of clandestine work in the context of clashing ideologies. There would be considerable truth in such a statement. Hunt *is* a fanatic right-wing anti-Communist left behind by the stream of history, and he could never overcome his obsession with the craft of intelligence. When the CIA no longer wanted him, he was ready to apply his compulsion and his intelligence skills to an assignment of domestic espionage and sabotage that the Nixon White House was able to offer him. When his once-beloved CIA tried to disassociate itself from him in the midst of the ensuing scandal, he turned on the Agency with total fury.

In September 1973, after his testimony before the Senate Watergate Committee (and represented by a new lawyer), Hunt suddenly asked Judge Sirica if he might change his plea to not guilty and moved for the dismissal of charges against him on the grounds that he had been misled by higher-ups to believe that his clandestine work was authorized from the very top. Having told the Senators that he was "crushed by the failure of my government to protect me and my family, as in the past it has always done for clandestine agents," Hunt now seemed to turn on the White House. Whether Hunt, indeed, began turning in state's evidence, Judge Sirica said on October 1 that he would be lenient in the final sentencing because a long term "would not only be unwarranted but unjust."

I asked a man who has known Hunt well over the years and who remains sympathetic to him to this day, what his reaction was upon learning of Hunt's role in Watergate. The answer was: "Incomprehension." I asked why. He said that Hunt was highly motivated, intelligent, humorous, always *au courant*, and despite his many personal failings did not seem to be the kind of person who would lend himself to situations that were so evidently unethical. Now this man, Hunt's friend, happens to be a highly ethical person in the old-fashioned conservative American way. And he has compassion for Hunt. We had a long talk, and one word kept recurring: incomprehension.

We must also, of course, look at Howard Hunt in the context of our times, and bear in mind the extraordinary cultural fears and inhibitions that forced President Nixon and his staff into a political offensive against a large segment of our nation, with top-secret intelligence plans and other cutouts from a *1984* fantasy. Hunt could have functioned only in such a power context.

But, in the end, Hunt's life was a chain of cruel ironies. He always craved power and importance. Briefly, he lived and acted in the shadow of White House power. Importance and recognition came in the form of Watergate's criminal notoriety. Strangely, Hunt became even more important to the White House—and to those who want to investigate the "horrors" of the early 1970s—after Watergate happened. He may hold national security secrets, and he may be safeguarding them as long as he remains fully protected—if that is possible for a man sentenced to long years in prison. Having always craved money, he may find this sense of protection in the blackmail payments which, for all we know, may make the difference between the survival and the erosion of the incumbent President. But, ironically, Hunt is rich already. The wealth comes from the $250,000 in flight insurance, to which he is entitled as sole beneficiary as a result of Dorothy's death. And, along with a recognition in the world of books—a belated recognition that came for all the wrong reasons—there are the book royalties. (Seventeen of his novels were reissued in 1973, as well as two new books.)

In a strange sense, Howard Hunt has a tragic place in our contemporary history. Unwittingly, he helped to trigger America's greatest political trauma of the century. This makes him important. But Howard Hunt is a man who has lost his way time after time and whose ultimate loyalty was to himself. His last novel opens with this epigraph:

It is in the political agent's interest to betray all the parties who use him and to work for them all at the same time, so that he may move freely and penetrate everywhere.